Does God Care When We Suffer?

Pearl Mc Lindly
12026 Haven Crest Street
Moorpark, Ca. 93021

Does God Care When We Suffer?

And Will He Do Anything About It?

Randy Becton

BAKER BOOK HOUSE
Grand Rapids, Michigan 49516

ISBN: 0-8010-0951-0

Printed in the United States of America

Contents

Foreword

One problem with all of the books on death and dying, someone has observed, is that the authors have never experienced what they are writing about. Many of us are fortunate enough to have the same problem when we write about suffering: we have not suffered very much. Randy Becton, however, knows all about suffering.

I first met Randy in the late 1960s when he enrolled in a class I was teaching at Harding Graduate School of Religion in Memphis, Tennessee. Then in 1971 we began to work closely together in the Herald of Truth ministry. This working relationship led to one of the most rewarding friendships of my life.

The personal struggle Randy recounts in the opening chapter of this book began to unfold soon after we began working together. Randy and Camilla have taught us a great deal as they have become "wounded healers" to thousands of people. Yet we have had many happy times together between the periods of acute suffering.

This book will not answer all of your questions about pain and suffering. But it will provide a resounding "Yes!" to the question posed by the title: "Does God care when we suffer?" And it will suggest reasons why we should believe God will help us with our pain.

The suffering of believers is heightened by our need to reconcile our personal pain with the goodness of God. If we did not believe God loves us, suffering would not be a profound philosophical or religious problem. We would simply say, "This is the way life is. What else can we expect?"

A child who has a cruel or uncaring parent and can honestly admit this can then go on to build his life without the parent. But the child who must pretend to himself that his father loves him, while deep in his heart he knows this is not true, may be crushed. Christians love God, trust him, and believe he is in control of the world. Yet how do they reconcile the existence of an almighty God of love who created the world with the tragic suffering they see all about them?

Randy Becton admits in the pages you are about to read that we cannot fully answer this question. But he argues convincingly that we know enough about God and his love to trust him. This trust and knowledge are built on what God did in Christ: he shared our limitations and our pain—even to the point of dying at the hands of his own creatures.

This book reminded me once again of the apostle Paul's response to his "thorn in the flesh": "And to keep me from being too elated by the abundance of revelations, a thorn was given me in the flesh, a messenger of Satan, to harass me, to keep me from being too elated. Three times I besought the Lord about this, that it should leave me; but he said to me, 'My grace is sufficient for you, for my power is made perfect in weakness.' I will all the more gladly boast of my weaknesses, that the power of Christ may rest upon me" (2 Cor. 12:7–9).

In an era when many counselors represent faith as an instant panacea for all ills, Paul's sober record of his experience is encouraging. If he had told us that after he prayed the thorn troubled him no more, we might have been discouraged by our own experience of continued suffering. And the same is true for the experiences the author recounts in this book.

Many of us have had a thorn in our life at one time or another. We have asked for release, but the thorn has not always disappeared. At times like that we can learn from Paul's experience—and from Randy's, as he reflects on his experience and what he has learned from God's Word.

Welcome to a caring, biblical treatment of our most pressing human problem!

HAROLD HAZELIP

Acknowledgments

I want to express my appreciation to Dr. Doug Shields, Dr. and Mrs. Eric Dahl and the University Christian Student Center at the University of Mississippi for their kind invitation to deliver this material first in their winter lecture series. Also, special thanks to Tricia Phillips for her careful editorial assistance and to my wife, Camilla, and my children Staci, Mark, Shana, and Shara for their patient encouragement on the long winter nights.

This book is dedicated to Randy Nicholson, whose life shows specific concern for those who suffer.

Introduction

In a short time I will be going to M.D. Anderson hospital for medical tests to determine if my cancer remains in remission. I've gone regularly since 1973. For much of that time I've reported to a clinic station next to the pediatric oncology section where I've seen many children as I've waited. As I sit and watch these young sufferers, I've often wondered, "How can we continue to believe in God if we deal with suffering children all day long?"

Dr. Jan van Eys is the head of pediatric oncology at M.D. Anderson. One day when I was browsing in the hospital library, I came across a book he had written about his experiences with terminally ill children and his faith in a loving God, *Humanity and Personhood: Personal Reaction to a World in Which Children Can Die.* I was deeply moved as I read the words of this thoughtful, caring doctor whose faith remained strong in the face of such tragic suffering. I became curious about how we sometimes choose to believe *in spite of* suffering and how at other times we choose not to believe any more *because of* suffering. I wondered about Dr. van Eys's faith and about my own.

This book explores suffering and faith, not theoretically, but personally. Does God care about our suffering and has He done—will He do—anything about it? The answer is very important to the sufferers I know and is equally important to me. This book represents my study of the problem of reconciling the fact of suffering with faith in a loving God and offers hopeful suggestions for both head and heart.

1

Suffering as Personal Experience

It may well be that the biggest question we ever ask is: "What is the meaning and purpose of human life?" Not far behind are questions about the origin of life (Is there a personal, creating God?) and the quality of life (What about human suffering?). To those who suffer, these questions are not distinct from each other; they are all part of the same question. Until we suffer, however, we may not raise these significant questions. When everything is well with us, we tend to suspend careful thought about the real values and issues of life. We are too busy with the pace and richness of "just living."

My Mother's Illness

Like many young persons, I cruised in this neutral gear through the first twenty-six years of my life. Although I experienced some personal disappointments and saw a number of

15

other people suffer, no serious problem directly attacked me or my family. At least none that I felt I couldn't handle.

That feeling was shattered in 1970 when we learned that my mother had breast cancer. This diagnosis was shocking for several reasons. My mother was only fifty years old, a beautiful and extremely active and healthy woman. She was the hub of our family. All of us—my father, older brother, my two younger sisters, and myself—depended on her intellectual, emotional, and spiritual strength. She was the organizing spirit behind our family gatherings, behind everything significant in the life of our family. We thought of her not only as indispensable but also indestructible. We were wrong.

At the time I was working on a graduate degree at Abilene Christian University in Abilene, Texas, and was employed as counselor for the national radio and television ministry, Herald of Truth. Mother required immediate surgery and then extensive radiation treatments over the course of the next few months. I flew to Nashville to be with her for the surgery, and while she was in the recovery room I sat in the hospital's medical library and read detailed articles about this ugly new reality called breast cancer.

That period of study and thought is seared in my memory. I felt personally violated, assaulted, invaded by this strange thing called cancer. I resented it, even became incredibly angry. *She doesn't deserve this,* I thought. *It just isn't fair.* Her life went in review before my mind. *She's had so many discouragements, God; it's wrong for you to let this happen to her.* I worried for her future; I worried for our family's future; I worried for *my* future. She was my friend, my counselor, my unique model, and even my hero.

When I returned home to my work, to my wife and our daughter Staci, I was still shaken by the new uncertainties that surrounded my mother. We kept in regular contact by phone, and I learned the painful, frustrating consequences that affect the body and mind of someone undergoing treatment for cancer.

During the next seven years, as Mother had other operations

for recurrent cancer and complications from her illness, I began to question the nature of suffering and a good God, seeking to reconcile my theological understanding with what was happening in the life of someone I loved so much.

During this time I came face to face with what one writer calls "life's imponderables"—those things we desperately want to know all about but can't seem to figure out very well. These have to do with God's ways, and Scripture says they are "past finding out" and that "the secret things belong to the Lord our God" (Rom. 11:33; Deut. 29:29 KJV). But I could find little peace and I exhausted myself trying to understand human suffering and the love of God.

Throughout this process God's silence bothered me just as it had bothered the Nobel-prize-winning writer Elie Wiesel. Wiesel, who was liberated from a Nazi prison camp, has spent his life writing about what happened to his people in the Holocaust. "I . . . want to know where God is. Why was God silent? I am a Jew and I come from a Hasidic upbringing. My disenchantment during the war was not with men but with God. What does He do? . . . what happened? Either God is present in history—in that case His presence must be felt—or I do not know."[1]

Questions are natural from the anguished heart. I will always remember the first letter that stopped me in my tracks in my work as a counselor. Although I received this more than sixteen years ago, these questions from a nurse in a Chicago suburb are still piercing ones.

Who said time heals all wounds? Who says God comforts? God is everywhere? Does He walk with me to the cemetery to visit the grave of my 6-year-old son who died of leukemia twelve years ago or the grave of my 18-year-old daughter who died of lymphoma two years ago?

Does He cry with me? What could He possibly do to ease the pain? Christ died for me? Who did they die for?

Does He know how it hurts to pray, pray to a God who is

merciful? Loving? Understanding? And on that judgment day
who is going to question whom?

I'll speak for all the bereaved. I work in a hospital. Does He
walk through the corridors to visit the sick, the dying? Is He
there to ease the pain, to wipe the tear? No! No! No!

Carol Straughn, herself a mother, commented on this letter:
"Truly there was nothing a mother could have done to deserve a
cancer death for her two children. Her cry of rage and despair
has rung out for thousands of years whenever the rule of 'happiness for the good and punishment for the bad' seemed to fail."

The cry of rage and despair continues. The year is 1987 and a
father from New Jersey has just written, telling me his daughter Becky, age seventeen, has died from leukemia.

My heart is as close to being broken and still alive as possible.
We had gone through 13 years of chemotherapy, had two re-
missions, and finally lost Becky to pneumonia...our only
child...I've seen so much suffering of innocent children for so
many years that the image of a loving God is too much for me to
accept any longer. Happiness is gone...I would really like to be
able to lean on my faith so much more than I can right now—but I
really don't expect anything now after how abandoned I feel by
my God. I am hurt real bad and don't expect to understand soon.
But I seem to want to keep on trying.

My Illness

We want so much to understand the cry of our own heart.
Even more, we long to reconcile our faith in a loving, personal
God with that cry. Yet we encounter the truth Solomon wrote:
"As you do not know the path of the wind...so you cannot
understand the work of God, the Maker of all things" (Eccl. 11:5
NIV). I had grappled with these questions as I sought to be an
effective people-helper in my work, and I found some comfort in
the faith of my mother during her suffering. However, my
questions were to become intensely personal and my own cry
was to become overwhelming in late October of 1973.

I had just been to Nashville for another of my mother's operations in September of that year. During the last week of October I went to our family doctor because of what I thought was a serious infection complicated by abdominal pain and swelling. After the examination he made immediate arrangements for me to be admitted into the hospital to begin a series of tests. Although he didn't alarm me, he implied that he suspected something serious. *in Oct 1973 — I learned*

The results of the lab tests were shocking: cancer of the *that I* lymph system. Now I became more than a sympathizer with *had* cancer patients; I became one of them. I underwent exploratory surgery, followed by a quick trip to M.D. Anderson Hospital and Tumor Institute in Houston, Texas, where I was evaluated and prepared for chemotherapy treatment. I was placed on the CHOP protocol, a combination of cancer-fighting chemicals given intravenously; these had powerful and even severe side effects.

I seemed to be dying physically day by day, and I wasn't doing much better in the emotional and spiritual battle. I struggled to live and at the same time struggled to keep my faith. My friend Glenn Owen observed about this conflict: "Faith does not always come from quiet contemplation or meditation. It is sometimes born among the raging of questions with no answers."[2]

Dr. Pat Harrell, himself a cancer patient, referred to this period of faith-searching as "religion born in a cry." That's exactly what it was for me. I was sick. I was scared. I was worried. Time has mercifully erased the terror of those days, but perhaps you'll understand the intensity of my thoughts through the following prayers written during those times:

I prayed

> The pain now goes beyond
> What is bearable
> Without you.
> The weariness and fear
> Are more than I can conquer
> Without you.

My eyesight is like a flickering
Candle,
And it's dark
Without you.
I confess:
I'm scared to death
Without you.
I have no more resources of faith
Without you.
So help me, God,
To take one step at a time
With you.
You are my only hope!

God, I'm frightened about
The uncertainty of my life—
It seems to be burning out.
The statistics are against me.
The advance of the disease
Is too far.
All I know to do is confess
That you are not limited by statistics.
You take the hopeless and
Renew their hope.
You are the living God.
How I yearn to be one
Of your healed children.

Father, how precious
Are my children:
Bright Staci;
Mark, in love with life;
Shana, newly exploring.
Depression visits me
Because they can't visit.
I need to touch them,
Hear their voices.
I'm shut away from them.
When I leave here, Father,
Help my arms, mind,

All of me
To participate fully
In their lives.
How much I love them—do you
Know how much? Of course you do.
I'm glad you understand
My longing to go home.

Father, I admit that I'm afraid
In a time when I ought to trust.
Many times fear conquers faith.
My mind plays tricks.
Horrors of my sickness
Are reruns—so often
They stalk me, chase me,
Finally exhaust me.
Relief comes when I feel your nearness.
Stay near, especially now as
Strong arms of fear press in.
I feel the security
Of a small child
Curling up
In his father's arms
In a terrible storm.
Let me sleep peacefully tonight.

O God, I cry and cry
Because my health
Leaves me helpless,
Totally dependent
On others,
On my family,
On you.
I confess
I'm incapable of working it out.
Helpless.
Without you I'm dead.
I don't want to be cowardly.
I just *so* want to live.
Death at thirty-two? Obscene.

My wife a young widow?
Please *no*, God.
It's so serious—
Not happening to someone else,
But to me.
I respond with fear,
Then faith,
Then anxiety,
Then trust,
Then fear again.
The emotional roller-coaster
Is undependable.
I *need* you so much, God.
Do you know that?

God, my Maker,
Hear my cry.
My body suffers with raging disease.
I'm confused,
Depressed,
Doubting your interest in me.
Why me?
Somehow the loneliness
I feel is cosmic.
No one is near.
No one cares.
Life goes smoothly on
For everyone but me.
And, O God, I'm dying.
I don't want to die now,
Not now.
Let me count to you all the reasons.
Do you hear me?
Will it matter?
If your hand doesn't stop the disease
I'm hopeless, unless you have mercy
To grant life.
If you choose, *will* it to be.
I cry to you, Lord.
Hear my cry, O God.

It's easy to hear the cry, isn't it? One of the cards I received in the hospital included a saying by the Indian philosopher Tagore: "Faith is the bird that feels the light and sings while the dawn is still dark." For me, it was a great struggle to feel the light and sing while the terrifying darkness hovered over me.

On occasion, the cosmic loneliness I prayed about still causes me to shudder. In an autobiographical book I wrote during my first year as a cancer patient, I pointed out that "the strongest single emotion I experienced was the loneliness caused by suffering and the uncertainty of facing the unknown."[3] I reevaluated my ideas about who God is. A Bible image for what I was experiencing comes from the apostle Peter when he spoke of those believers to whom he wrote who were facing "the fiery ordeal" (1 Peter 4:12).

I had always believed that a Christian did not hope without reason. Christians, as Martin Marty points out, always "hope for, hope in, hope that, [a Christian] hopes in God, therefore, everything turns on the character of the living God."[4] The psalmist would say of God, "My hope is in you" (Ps. 39:7 NIV). I tested my belief about God, seeking to reassure myself that he was near me, that he was someone I could trust with this horrible dilemma, that he was someone who really cared. Of course, my deepest desire was self-serving. I wanted God to care about my life enough to do what I wanted—restore it!

I knew that God owed me nothing. Everything I was, possessed, and hoped for was bound up in his graciousness. But I was testing whether or not he was my heavenly Father and really cared about me. I was trying so hard to believe he cared. I tried to make my fears fade into his promises so that my hope would be secure and my trust could provide me peace. I lived in the Psalms. "The Lord is near to the brokenhearted, and saves the crushed in spirit" (Ps. 34:18). I would pray, "Lord, help me believe that."

I was certain, because of the Psalms, that I could trust God with the full range of my human emotions. What I did not know was that this trust is a daily decision and is not a secure possession to be taken for granted. As Martin Marty asks, can you really sing "The Lord is my strength and my shield; in him

my heart trusts" (Ps. 28:7) when later you may have to ask – as I
did when diagnosed in 1981 with a recurrence of cancer – "Why,
O God, after a remission of disease, is it allowed to come back
relentlessly?"[5]

But   From November 1973 until the spring of 1974 I had chemotherapy to fight the cancer. In the spring check-up, the doctor
told me he thought I was in remission from the cancer. I continued with the treatments with a deep sense of relief. I had lost
my hair, lost substantial weight, but I felt that I might have a
chance to live. I was excited about the possibility of returning to
work and reestablishing some normalcy in our family life. (Our
three children were all under five years of age, and a major fear
in the early months of my illness was that my wife would be left,
a young widow of twenty-eight, with three small children and
sadly inadequate finances.)

My Second Illness

During the years from 1974 until 1981 I had two surgeries for
intestinal obstructions and one for an abdominal abscess. Before these surgeries, however, I was often in severe pain, and I
experienced constant frustration because doctors could not lo-
cate the cause. They gave me pain medicine, but I endured long
periods of confusion because some of the cancer doctors did not
want to deal with the abdominal distress. Finally, the obstructions were found and repaired.

Then, my world fell apart. In the spring of 1981 a CAT scan
discovered lymphoma (lymph cancer) again. I was hospitalized
in Houston and once more began chemotherapy. This time the
children were old enough to understand the threat. The old
emotional and spiritual battles were complicated by two new
problems: the children's understanding and needs and the news
that I would be hospitalized for chemotherapy one week out of
three for the entire year. A year of our lives was to be totally
disrupted.

That year, my faith was severely tested. This time I felt God
did not love me. I also could not understand why I had to

I had several ups and downs

experience this pain and loneliness a second time. It was a year
of impatience.

Larry Richards, in *When It Hurts Too Much to Wait*, says that
although we must wait on God's timetable, "He remains the one
behind our circumstances . . . When the pain of waiting makes
us doubt the reality of God's love," we can look to Jesus and
because we are bonded to him "we can be assured of His commitment to us." The "anchor" of our relationship with God is not
"our subjective feelings" but the "reality of His love for us."[6]

I spent a year trying to convince myself that this was true. It
seemed easy for someone else to say, "God's timing, even when
the waiting is long and painful, never means abandonment."[7]
But for myself, I found it incredibly hard to believe his love
surrounded me. This problem was not mine alone; it's ageless.
The psalmist cried, "Why have you abandoned me?" And those
six million or more Jews who died during the Holocaust echoed
this. Philip Yancey, writing about the concentration camps,
observed:

> Religious hope did not survive for everyone. To some, the tragedy
> of the camps was final proof that God did not care about the
> human plight. But to others . . . religious faith was a hope that
> could not be extinguished . . . God could be hoped for forever,
> even though he seemed very distant at the time.[8]

Again, by the grace of God, I survived and was pronounced in
remission. From 1981 until the present my medical checkups
have shown no evidence of malignancy. No cancer. I'm so thankful. God has restored my health not once, but twice.

Brother to Sufferers

My friend Landon Saunders was a unique gift from God
during my first illness. He was a visible reminder of the love of
God and a tangible link to that love. His touch in my life spoke
to me of God's love. I recall hearing someone say that if you
want people to know the love of God, they must experience it
through human touch. That was true for me in Landon's touch.

From the time of my first diagnosis people around the nation knew about me. This was true in part because Landon was so well-known as the premier young speaker among Churches of Christ—at special events, and in the whole fellowship. Also, I was visible in the church because of my association with Herald of Truth, the only national radio and television outreach in the Churches of Christ. I worked closely with the most well-known and loved preacher at that time in the Churches of Christ, Dr. Batsell Barrett Baxter. As a result of all this, churches everywhere sent word that they were praying for me. People phoned with words of encouragement, and college students from almost every state wrote notes, cards, and letters wishing for me full recovery. It was a deeply compassionate outpouring.

Occasionally these callers and letter writers told me of other cancer sufferers whom they were encouraging. Because I had begun to write about my experiences, these people related their experiences to me as if we were close friends. Many letters and notes were from former patients. Some were doing well; others still struggled; most wanted to either offer or receive encouragement.

Because my life was being spared, I felt a strong tug to help these people. I reasoned that (a) I knew something about "trials," and (b) I had been given a second chance. Maybe it was for just this kind of work that I'd been spared. After a brief period of not wanting to think about the gruesome experience of cancer, I launched into a letter-writing and encouragement ministry. I began with articles like "You're Not Alone"—a message of hope to Christians struggling with cancer, and "We're Fellow Strugglers"—a message of hope to non-Christians with cancer.

I felt a close kinship to these people who were being told, "You have cancer." I knew some of the things they would experience, and I knew how hard it probably would be. I felt that I could empathize and that I could sincerely and honestly relate to them. The possibility that I might be used to encourage some of them and maybe lessen their burden was exciting. When my articles became printed booklets, more and more

I began helping others through my booklets.

The response was overwhelming

people wrote, sharing their stories and requesting more reading material.

By 1978 Camilla and I could not handle the volume of correspondence by ourselves, so we sought to organize a sensitive group of volunteers to help us. We saw the value of creating a non-profit group, the Caring Cancer Ministry, to try to help as many cancer patients and their families as possible. We were responding to needy people as best we could to help them deal with the emotional and spiritual challenges that are a part of the cancer experience.

One night Camilla and I participated in a New York City teleconference sponsored by the Heartbeat ministry, an outreach founded and headed by Landon Saunders. We were being broadcast to Nashville, Dallas, and Houston. In introducing me, Landon used a quote that warmed my heart—and still does. I share it now because it reminds me of why I am involved in a caring ministry to cancer patients and their families:

> Whoever among us has,
> Through personal experience,
> Learned what pain and
> Suffering really are,
> Belongs no more
> To himself alone.
> He is the brother of all who suffer.[9]

We then organized the

I would like very much to be the brother to all who suffer. From the time it was started through 1986, the Caring Ministry has distributed over 100,000 booklets, books, tapes, and posters to the suffering and to those who seek to meet their needs. It's a small but not insignificant beginning.

Lewis Smedes says, "When you hurt with hurting people, you are dancing to the rhythm of God."[10]

I am trying to dance to that rhythm. Trying to live not for myself any longer, but for my God. And because my face is set in that direction, I try to "think of all who suffer as if [I] shared their pain" (*Phillips*).

2

Why Is There Suffering in the World?

Of the thousands of letters I've received from people who suffer, I would estimate that less than twenty have actually asked *why* there is suffering in the world. Yet scores and scores of them ask such questions as "How can I cope with my suffering?" "Where is God when it hurts?" "When will suffering end?"

I think this is a good indication that most people's concern about suffering is practical, not theoretical. They want to know how to handle their suffering and how to relate it to their belief in the goodness, power, and wisdom of God. Dr. Paul Schilling, long-time professor at Boston University, reminds us that we deal with "the anguish of real people...the suffering that raises the troublesome, theoretical questions occurs in concrete experience."[1]

In fact, it is usually those who are not suffering who are most interested in the theoretical. Despite this, there is value in exploring what we can know about why suffering exists.

Our Questions Lead Us to God

When we hear the word *suffering*, most of us automatically think of evil; the word conjures up all the forces or people associated with that which actively opposes our good. Not all evil involves suffering, but "we know evil primarily as suffering."[2]

Evil seems to be an abstract concept, while suffering concerns concrete experience. When we speak of suffering, we usually refer to physical or mental pain, some type of devastating loss, distress, or injury. Suffering is a personal experience and each person defines it for himself or herself. People can show you the scars suffering leaves on their lives.

Of the hard "why" questions, "why is there suffering?" may be the hardest. This is probably because it not only attacks us personally, but also because whenever the question is raised, the question of God's part in suffering follows close behind. "The theologians of every generation rethink the paradox of a loving and provident God who allows so much misery and anguish."[3]

Dr. Joseph Fichter, professor of sociology at Loyola University in New Orleans, writes: "There is no scientific or causal-historical answer to the question, 'Why must there be suffering in the world?' The specific cause of a specific pain could be sometimes detected, but the larger answer could not be found at the level of natural logic and scientific causality."[4]

Fichter adds that behavioral scientists assume that various primitive people have raised the issue to the realm of supernatural religion.[5] We think of God so quickly because we're aware of forces over which we have limited or no control; we sense our mortality and perhaps intuitively believe in a higher creative power; or we seek relief so desperately that we look outside ourselves.

The evil of man's inhumanity to his fellow man causes great suffering. However, we are much more puzzled by what Clifford

Geertz calls "morally undeserved"[6] suffering: the child born with a deformity; the person maimed through a freak accident; the young adult with a terminal disease. We know that wars are started in the minds of human beings who hate or seek domination. But even then we want to know why God "allows" them in light of the fact that so many innocent people suffer. We are desperate for the *meaning* behind all this. We seek someone to blame or to deliver us, and that always leads to our view of God.

Views of Believers and Unbelievers

I don't know who gets angrier with God, believers or un-believers, but I suspect those who believe in a personal, loving God have the most difficulty. C. S. Lewis, a devout believer, married late and then helplessly watched as his wife, Joy, died. In *A Grief Observed*, he asks:

> Meanwhile, where is God? This is one of the most disquieting symptoms. When you are happy, so happy that you have no sense of needing Him, if you turn to Him then in praise, you will be welcomed with open arms. But to go to Him when your need is desperate, when all other help is vain and what do you find? A door slammed in your face, and a sound of bolting and double bolting on the inside. After that, silence. You may as well turn away.[7]

To the question, "Where is God when it hurts?" Philip Yancey says, "It's a problem that won't go away."[8] Suffering is as likely to produce a stronger faith as it is to sow agnosticism, says Yancey, and what makes the difference is tied up in the choice of the one who suffers. (We'll deal more with that later.) Yancey claims to know a key to unlock the why of suffering: "My anger and bitterness against God have subsided as I've come to realize why He allows this bleeding world."[9] He believes the key is to enter the world of suffering people, study their answers by examining their faith, and then read Scripture carefully to see what God is up to in the world: "My anger about pain has melted mostly for one reason: I have come to know God."[10]

Yancey believes that God has designed a pain system in this world for our benefit—principally to turn us away from self-interest, which leads only to death, toward God. Then as humanity cries out about this blemished and imperfect world, they are able to hear God's message: that he has rescued us from this misery by sharing our suffering personally, by becoming one of us, and that he has prepared a new life where suffering will be ended. Yancey's conclusion: Pain turns us to God. In his view, this is probably the most accurate, succinct summary of the role of suffering, and he works out this thesis using Scripture and stories of sufferers. His is not a new message. The most important question is: Is it true? And does it speak authentically to suffering people?[11]

Former college president, Paul Billheimer, comes at the problem of suffering a little differently. In his *Don't Waste Your Sorrows*, he argues that "from all eternity suffering is inherent in God's economy (universe)." In his reasoning "God is the supreme sufferer in the universe" because there was no suffering in the created order until mankind exercised his freedom to disobey the Creator. The result of this free exercise of the human will to rebel was sin, the beginning of all suffering in the human realm.[12]

The cornerstone of the universe, in Billheimer's view, is not the reality of human suffering but the operating principle of suffering love. The foremost sign of man's suffering is his sinfulness which caused him to die. God is agape love and gives himself willingly for man's deliverance from this suffering through Jesus' death. For Billheimer, life's "painful circumstances" are planned by God—he's actively in the middle of them—to bring us to himself.[13]

Brian Hebblethwaite is a lecturer in divinity at Queens College in Cambridge, England. His *Evil, Suffering and Religion* describes different answers offered in various religions where belief in *a* God is central.[14]

In Buddhism, for example, there is no interest in the why of suffering; instead, the emphasis is on coping through a serene resignation and self-sacrifice. In Chinese Taoism believers are similarly urged to yield themselves passively to a mysterious universal harmony rather than resist through questioning. In contrast, Judaism, Islam, and Christianity all have a doctrine of creation in which humans come into being and exist in a relationship to a God who exercises his creative will. In these religions evil does not exist on its own (dualism) but is a disturbance or aberration of what is inherently good (that is, the created world).

In Christianity, the personification of evil is Satan, an angel who rebelled against God. In Genesis he tempts Eve leading to her rebellion and sin and, consequently, her suffering. In the Book of Job, he is allowed to test humans. In Matthew, the devil even tempts Jesus. The devil's presence causes much suffering. The apostle John suggests the existence of a kingdom of darkness, while Paul points out that Satan is "the prince of the power of the air" (Eph. 2:2).

The reality of Satan suggests a strong connection between his presence and a corresponding amount of misery and suffering in people's lives. I'll quickly add that human free will seems intact in Scripture and, without question, biblical writers believe God's power prevails overall and that ultimately God triumphs. Nevertheless, the troublesome reality of Satan and his activity is present in the human realm.

Answering the Why

Hebblethwaite mentions five answers to the why question about suffering.

1. *Suffering is divine punishment.* Mankind is guilty and therefore deserving of punishment. There is no question that examples of divine reward and punishment are present as Old Testament writers discuss the kings of Israel and Judah and the people of God, but there are also instances of the innocent suffering (for example, Job and Jesus).

2. *Suffering is a divine test or trial of faith.* God permits Satan to test his servant Job, and in this way suffering is seen as a necessary process to develop character. "It is for discipline that you have to endure. God is treating you as sons; for what son is there whom his father does not discipline" (Heb. 12:7).

Christian theologians have enjoyed using soul-making or the building of character or endurance as an answer to why.[15] Although this may be valid as a partial answer, we must caution ourselves against the temptation to say that people can't be strong of character or sacrificial in spirit without large doses of human misery. This answer also is inadequate to deal with such things as natural disasters and human slaughter.

3. *Suffering is part of the gift of human freedom.* To love God properly we have to be created free to choose him. Persons choose; puppets react to strings. Moral evil and its result, suffering, are necessary components of a world of persons. Unfortunately, only human wickedness is best explained by human "wrong" choices. (How did Catherine's husband know he should not have been on Oceanside highway when the rocks fell and crushed his car?)

4. *Suffering is part of the nature and function of the physical world.* The universe functions according to certain laws that govern its well-being. Natural causes like floods, droughts, and earthquakes hurt many innocent people. The energies and powers in the physical properties of the universe are either God-given, as Christians believe, or somehow have a mind of their own. Hebblethwaite poses the question here: "Why does God create a physical world which, for all its wonders and beauties, can cause untold harm to sentient beings?" He answers this by saying that "the properties of nature which cause harm to creatures are precisely the same fundamental properties which make possible an organic world of growth and change, the context of personal being and development."[16]

5. *Suffering is creation in process.* Since creation is an ongoing process leading to a future goal, there is suffering now. It's just the price we pay. This view rejects the idea that the world operates as a cycle of growth and decay. Persons are seen

as minor players in a drama that is really about an impersonal, physical world.

C. J. Ducasse in *A Philosophical Scrutiny of Religion* identifies four classes of evil: *physical*—diseases or pain associated with the human body and its limitations and the forces in the natural universe; *psychological*—all the states of mind that create suffering such as loneliness, anxiety, fear, and rejection; *moral*—all those negative character traits such as selfishness, greed, malice, hatred, and cruelty; and *intellectual*—including irrational behavior, bad judgment, and stupidity."[17]

Langdon Gilkey thinks a division between "manageable" (those things subject to human control) and "unmanageable" (those things, like natural disasters and death, outside of human control) is helpful.[18] But even if we were to believe that much more suffering springs from human beings themselves than from the forces of nature, we would still have to agree with C. S. Lewis: "Even if all suffering were man-made, we should like to know the reason for the enormous permission to torture their fellows which God gives to the worse of men."[19]

The Need to Settle the Question of a Personal God

Gilkey writes that while unbelievers seek to understand the why and ask how suffering can be overcome, the person of faith asks: "Is there a creator and sovereign being who rules over these powers that rule over us?"[20]

Christians deal best with the why of human suffering in relation to "*Who* is my God?" They see God as the source of good and, historically, have sought to understand God's relationship to the existence of evil in the form of human suffering. The power and extent of suffering notwithstanding, believers assert that somehow God is involved.

This need for a personal, caring God is exemplified by the experience of a college friend of mine from my hometown. He graduated with honors in foreign language and history and went on to graduate school, where I lost track of him for several years. Then one holiday time we encountered each other back in our hometown. As we caught up on what had been happening during the years since we'd last seen each other, he told me about his disillusionment with life and faith and his search for meaning. He had been reading Walter Kaufmann's book, *The Faith of a Heretic*, and had concluded he could no longer believe in God.

His honesty and earnestness were impressive. But the thing that struck me most was his sadness over his conclusion, for he told me that much of the meaning had gone out of his life. He urged me to read Kaufmann's book. He knew I had struggled with cancer and felt that the author's discussion of human suffering might be helpful to me.

A number of months later my phone rang. It was my friend's wife calling to tell me he was dead. He had committed suicide. According to the note he left his wife, it was evident that when the intellectual argument of a philosopher eroded his confidence in a personal, caring God, despair took over – the ultimate despair.

A Word About Unbelievers and Suffering

Dr. Walter Kaufmann, whose *Faith of a Heretic* devastated my friend, taught philosophy for more than twenty-five years at Princeton. He wrote: "The problem of suffering is of crucial importance because it shows that the God of popular theism does not exist...the perplexing problem of suffering...[is] rendered insolvable – unless either the traditional belief in God's boundless power or the belief in His perfect justice and mercy is abandoned. Short of that, only pseudo-solutions are possible."[21]

Kaufmann's aggressive, accusatory style ridicules the God of the Bible, but he merely built on those who went before him.

Karl Marx, Friedrich Nietzsche, and Sigmund Freud were three of the foremost atheists in the modern era who have hammered at the notion of a personal, caring God in the face of human suffering. They saw human beings as overwhelmed by nature, living in a world that spares them no sufferings. Thus, they said, humans have invented God for themselves because they need consolation. In *The Sources of Modern Atheism*, French philosopher and theologian Marcel Neusch, writes that for Marx, Nietzche, and Freud "God's essential function" is to provide men with a faith to sustain them and a hope to console them.[22]

Marx saw faith in God as seeking for a "heart in a heartless world." Freud said we look to God for a "palliative measure" in a world that "brings us too many pains" and this helps us put up with an "unbearable life." Their view is that faith is "the cry of a ravaged heart" and that a God who arises out of suffering people's need is not a very solid God. They also saw heaven as a projection of need because humanity seeks for a time when justice will finally overcome all the injustices suffering has caused in this world.[23]

Neusch points out that while they rejected a God of need, they were "ignorant of the God of 'desire': the God who freely gives himself and, far from forcing himself on human beings, calls upon them to freely give themselves."[24]

Believers and Unbelievers Confront Silence

Because of unbelievers who see the reality of human misery and sincerely try to grapple with it in light of their understanding of the world and religion, but reach the end of the power of their logic, we also must ask our questions honestly.

First, *it's helpful to admit that there is a hiddenness with God.* If he doesn't take the initiative in making himself known—both his character and intentions—we only know him as *power* not as *person* (see Luke 10:21; 1 Cor. 1:17–25). We would be limited to religious speculation no matter how much we desired to know. "We know God through God and only through God."[25] He is a God of revelation; that's why the trustworthiness and reliability of the Bible is so important.

Second, *because God must reveal himself, it is impossible to start with suffering and get to God through reasoning alone. The*

best understanding of suffering comes after we have begun with
the God who revealed himself in Jesus Christ. I agree with Sören
Kierkegaard that reason must be informed by a faith that
responds to who God says he is. We decide whether we believe
God. It is our decision whether or not to trust.

If atheism proves anything, it proves the inability of man to
use reason to understand suffering or God. Of course, when I
say that we must start with God, I must go on to say that
Scripture makes Jesus Christ our starting point in understanding God in a personal way. Human life and human suffering is
understandable only when we seek to understand God as he is
revealed in Jesus Christ. Our experiences of suffering make us
cry out for meaning, but that meaning will come only as we
come to understand who we are in relation to God.

In reality, when God reveals himself, he is revealing everything about us and about our suffering. Knowledge of ourselves
and our situation is his gift to us. Someone has suggested that if
we come to suffering *with* faith, we understand suffering far
better than if we come to suffering looking for faith. When we
understand God better, we understand better "the coherence of
the world, but also why the world is shot through with
questions."[26]

Atheists, wrong though they are, have the right to decide
that the world is absurd and all things end in nothingness
(nihilism). Neusch says: "The trust which an atheist has in the
world and in life is in fact without a foundation. In refusing to
assign an ultimate foundation and an ultimate meaning he
prevents himself from satisfactorily explaining reality...He
may give his life a partial meaning by a heroic effort to make it
bear fruit in time, but sooner or later he is compelled to acknowledge the absence of meaning."[27]

And let's remember that the enormous problem atheists
have in explaining good may equal the challenge believers have
in answering for bad. When we say yes to God as our foundation
and purpose, we bring unity, value, and meaning to our life. Of
course, that doesn't mean we understand *all*—and we quickly

add that a large measure of modesty and humility about what we don't know is wise, even essential.

The Czechoslovakian philosopher Machovec stated bluntly, "I can't combine faith in God with Auschwitz."[28] A character in Peter DeVries's *The Blood of the Lamb* said to a sick friend when she asked him to pray, "That would mean the one I was addressing had done this to you to begin with."[29] He adds: "I simply mean that asking Him to cure you—or me, or anybody—implies a personal being who arbitrarily does us this dirt. The prayer then is a plea to have a heart. To knock it off. I find the thought repulsive. I prefer to think we're the victims of chance to dignifying any such force with the name of providence!"[30]

Believers respond that the supreme instance of God's silence in the presence of unjust suffering was when he watched his only son, Jesus, scorned, mistreated, and unjustly crucified. Who hasn't cried out in our own hour of distress, "Lord, tell us the plan; give us the sign." The psalmist asked long ago, "Why, O Lord, do you stand far off? Why do you hide yourself in times of trouble?" (Ps. 10:1 NIV). And Habbakuk the prophet asked God, "Why are you silent while the wicked swallow up those more righteous than themselves?" (Hab. 1:13 NIV).

When I was a college student in Tennessee, I was privileged to live near three of the finest black institutions of higher learning in this country: Meharry Medical College, Tennessee State University, and Fisk University. This was during the 1960s and I developed a perspective of appreciation for the life and work of Martin Luther King, Jr. In one of his sermons he asked, "Why does the Holy One of Israel permit white people to oppress helpless black people when the Scripture says God came in Jesus Christ to set the captives free?"[31] I was a sophomore in college then and more unaware than I should have been of the suffering people in my city wondering about the silence of God.

The most common kind of psalm found in the Book of Psalms is the lament, a kind of "sufferer's cry" out to a God he trusts will hear him and will answer. People of Israel would "appeal to

God's compassion to intervene and change a desperate situation."[32] Bernhard Anderson observes: "The psalmists are not like Greek tragedians who portray a no-exit situation of fate or necessity; rather they raise a cry out of the depths in the confidence that God has the power to lift a person out of the 'miry bog' and to set one's feet upon a rock. (Ps. 40:1–3)."[33]

The point here is that people of faith have *always* had to wait. They've found themselves living "in the interim between God's promise and the fulfillment of the promise." This interim is a time when faith is really tested because "there are no unambiguous proofs that God has spoken and that God is in control of the human situation."[34] George Buttrick in his well-received *God, Pain and Evil* reminded readers that we all deal personally rather than theoretically with suffering.[35] Everyone's soul has its own dark nights.

One of the assumptions I make in my consideration of suffering is that *because* God is a God of personal love and purpose, he has communicated his intention for humanity through his self-revelation in Jesus Christ. I don't pretend to approach suffering from any other vantage point. If God's creative purpose with humans involves relationship (fellowship) with them in the fulfillment of his purpose, then he will not leave them drifting or wondering about the real meaning of their being human.

One facet of God's nature, I'm firmly convinced, is his *initiative*. He sheds light on our suffering because we matter to him. In short, I believe the Bible lays out the data about God's self-disclosure persuasively and convincingly. It helps us get a good grasp on the human condition, giving us the best possible understanding of human suffering. Some people ask: If God wants to be known so badly, why do so many—over so many years—lament his silence or absence? The answer may lie in finding out more about human sinfulness.

Attempts by man to vindicate the justice or righteousness of a God who allows human suffering are called *theodices*. There have been many theodices through the centuries. One deserving of mention is that there is profound *mystery* both in suffering and in faith. Some folk religions emphasize "a wheel of fortune" concept that suggests that people are victims of circumstance, sometimes doing well, sometimes not. In this view there is some hidden wheel of fortune that determines these things and man's best chance to cope is resignation—don't fight the system. This view argues that man's purposes are obscure and that he can learn nothing for sure of his origin, purpose, or destiny.

Voltaire's Candide concludes that all we can do is "cultivate our garden" because the world is a mysterious place and its purposes are unknowable. Charles Darwin's indecision between chance and design led him to conclude also that there were mysteries too difficult to harmonize: "I cannot persuade myself that a beneficent and omnipotent God would have designedly created [a butterfly from a caterpillar]. . .I see no necessity in the belief that the eye was expressly designed."[36]

While some people confront mystery with puzzlement and wonder, others trust that a God with good purposes is in control of human events. When bad things happen, they say that God has some purpose for this that they cannot see, and they accept it without question. This theology of *quiet resignation* goes something like this: "What has happened is awful, but it must be a part of God's plan. Although I can't understand his purpose, I must have faith and do my part and God will see me through." Ann Landers reflected this in her answer to a lady: "You must believe that God in His infinite wisdom had a reason—not known to you now, but it is there."[37]

Others, like Father Jamme, *actively trust*. Father Jamme was a Belgian priest, who spent thirty-five years researching an obscure civilization in Yemen seeking to recover their language and history. Seven days a week, in the deserts of Yemen and Turkey, he searched for inscriptions and records in order to build a dictionary of this ancient culture. Then in the fall of 1975 a fire destroyed most of his life's work. His response: "I know there is a great lesson in this. But I don't know what it is. What He wanted me to learn, I do not know. That He had a good reason, there is no doubt."[38] He went back to his work, confident that God's purposes were being worked out, even in the face of his profound loss.

We must be careful, however, not to refer to all suffering as God's will. This is misleading, even wrong. It is one thing to say that God is working his will for us in a certain event; it is quite another to say that God planned the event.

3

The Meaning
of Suffering

$\mathbf{I}$n attempting to examine the meaning of suffering, I want to further explore several of the answers to the "why" that seem most prevalent today. Two of the oldest answers are that suffering is God's judgment on man's sin and that God sends suffering in order that we may grow spiritually.

Suffering as Judgment

In *The Mystery of Pain*, Paul Lindell says: "Natural evil and pain are always the visible sign of God's 'No!' which He pronounced on creation and on man because of the sinful alienation of man from God. Ever since the gate to the garden was shut and the angel of the Lord was placed there to guard it with a flaming sword—ever since that day the earth has been filled with violence and thistles, pain and disorder, decay and despair...God has decided it shall be so."[1]

Lindell traces the beginning of humanity's suffering to

Adam's and Eve's decision to rebel and disobey in the Garden of Eden. Because of their disobedience, God pronounced a curse of suffering on them. "I will multiply your pain in childbearing... cursed is the ground because of you; in toil you shall eat of it all the days of your life; thorns and thistles it shall bring forth to you... In the sweat of your face you shall eat bread till you return to the ground" (Gen. 3:16–19). Thus, pain in childbirth and hard manual labor are seen as suffering resulting from man's rebellion. "Adam's choice [his sin] opened a 'Pandora's box' of suffering for mankind... physical, spiritual, social, psychological, ecological."[2]

In the days of Noah, God sent the flood to destroy everything because of man's love for wrongdoing. When Joseph's brothers sold him into slavery, God punished them with a severe famine. Later, the prophets underlined the fact that God was the righteous judge and that the many forms of suffering the people were experiencing (drought, pestilence, enemy invasion) were the consequences of their sin.

Dr. Warren McWilliams says we can't escape or explain away the "retributive principle that most suffering is the penalty for sin."[3] When the people in the prophet Jeremiah's day oppressed aliens, widows, and orphans; ignored the poor; and structured their business on greed and dishonesty, they were told to repent or the Babylonians would invade, destroying them and ruining their land as God's punishment. They would be consumed "by the sword, by famine, and by pestilence" (Jer. 14:12; 32:36; 38:2).

Erhard Gerstenberger and Wolfgang Schrage point out that this divine "judicial proceeding" was likely the first thing the people of Israel thought about when misfortune came to them. In this way, God's punishment had educational value: "According to the Israelite view, however, it is only through his own pain that man learns to stay within his limits and thereby to provide a basis for his happiness."[4]

This answer contains a major problem, however, for while some suffering is caused by sin, not all suffering is. Nor does it fully explain why the righteous or "innocent" suffer. The

Psalms and the Book of Job seem to indicate that sooner or later wicked people will suffer for what they do; that freedom from suffering indicates divine favor; but also that sometimes the righteous do suffer and that though we don't understand this, God does.

We must also remember to make a distinction between suffering caused by natural disasters and suffering caused by sin. It's largely true that injustice produces adversity and it's generally true that we reap what we sow, although not always. However, it's not true that all suffering is the result of sin. Unfortunately, these distinctions may be so fine that they are lost on us when we hurt and want to know why.

Mr. Nickles in Archibald MacLeish's play *J.B.* thought the explanation for all this was simple: "If God is God, He is not good. If God is good, He is not God."[5] He didn't believe God could rule judiciously and punish and still be good.

This brings us to a point about which I want to be very honest: If you have not made the decision to place your life under the control of this God being described as sovereign and just as well as loving and giving, then you will likely reject as incredible his role as judge over all the earth.

Suffering as Growth

The concept of suffering as an agent of growth is also a long-standing answer to the "why." Irenaeus, an early church father, believed that God wanted Christians to accept the events of their lives in "a teachable spirit, as means whereby His creative purpose for us is fulfilled."[6]

The poet John Keats, in sending a letter to his brother and sister, tried to give a rationale for the hardships they were experiencing. He described life as a kind of school for the molding of character, "a vale of soul-making."[7]

In more recent years many spiritual leaders and theologians have expressed similar sentiments. For example, Rabbi Hirshel Jaffe takes this approach in describing his experience with cancer: "This has been a real learning experience for me . . .

some people say God allows us to suffer so we can learn from it. I think I'm beginning to agree with that. Instead of wondering, 'Why me, why did this happen to me?' you can say . . . 'What can I do with it?'. . . it's whether you use the painful experience for enrichment or for embitterment."[8]

When speaker and writer Vance Havner lost his wife, he considered it a great spiritual testing. He said, "I had been for many years relatively free from trouble, grief, and distress and sometimes I wondered that I had known so little of that adversity that indicates our sonship."[9]

Dr. Walter Kaiser, Jr., writes:

> It is necessary to place alongside retributive suffering the complementary principle of *educational* or *disciplinary* suffering. While God must often punish His people for their sins, a corollary emerged in the process of divine revelation; God often afflicted His people for the purpose of teaching them. "My son," urged Solomon in Proverbs 3:11, "do not despise the chastening (musar) of the Lord, do not be weary of His reproof." Therefore, the man or woman whom God loved He chastened and corrected often through pain, suffering, and anguish."[10]

Paul Schilling refers to Abraham's offering of Isaac in establishing the fact that "recurrent in the biblical writings are two interrelated themes: (1) Our sufferings serve to sometimes test our faith; (2) Our trials are disciplines designed to purify character."[11]

John Hick writes that we know God's character and purpose because of "his incarnation in Jesus Christ." Hick believes God is "fashioning souls," molding men into the image of Jesus, his son.[12] However, as Schilling observes, the objection comes that "some obstacles and calamities have the opposite effect," producing suffering so intense and heavy that resentment, rebellion, and even character disintegrate.[13] Hick admits that this is an insoluble problem.

I've always been cautious about offering the possibilities for growth to someone who is suffering intensely. I feel it borders on insensitivity. While few of us would deny that people have grown through certain kinds of suffering in their lives, does this in itself give us the *reason* for suffering? Perhaps the key is that, as in so many things, this concept is only part of the answer and therefore only partially helpful.

Suffering as the Result of the Physical Order

Scripture tells us that God "makes his sun rise on the evil and on the good, and sends rain on the just and the unjust" (Matt. 5:45). This verse refers to the regularity and constancy of nature, the natural laws that are part of God's created order, and the fact that all creatures are subject to those laws.

Believers see these laws as part of the framework provided by a loving God—until they want him to intervene and set aside some natural law because its normal function puts them in jeopardy. Geological processes are fine until we face earth quakes and volcanoes. Gravity is great until we step too close to the edge of a cliff.

When this happens we realize that sun and rain produce difficulties as well as blessings. And this in turn helps us understand some of the random undeserved suffering in our world. An all-powerful God whose created order is structured to accomplish his good purposes does not go around rearranging these laws whenever we purposely or unknowingly cross one of them.

God has declared that he is not outside of and aloof from his created order; instead, he is inside and benevolent to it. That's why the word *incarnation* is so valuable. Paul says, "He is before all things, and in him all things hold together" (Col. 1:17).

Schilling concludes that "the eternal spirit whose redemptive love acted incomparably in a particular person also works creatively throughout the natural and historical orders . . . [and this helps us by declaring] if the whole world is God's deed, its occasions of suffering . . . somehow fall within his responsibility

...[and] portrays Him as directly and intimately involved in the anguish of His creatures."[14]

God doesn't set aside the regular patterns of his natural order to eliminate the suffering that is part of its functioning. His order has loving purposes and one of these is "the formation of persons for fellowship withGod".[15]

Sheldon Vanauken's essay "It Was God's Will" imagines a life devoid of any human act that has been freely generated. He depicts God stepping in and stopping every negative thought or destructive act:

> A Nazi guard turns the gas on the naked, huddled victims. But the people don't clutch their throats at all. The walls of the chamber fall down. The guards draw their guns and fire, but God catches the bullets with His hand.
>
> A submarine fires his missiles at the cruiser. God reaches into the water and deflects them away safely.
>
> A rapist prepares to assault his victim, but finds an invisible wall between him and her.
>
> A woman, used to screaming at her incompetent husband, suddenly finds herself voiceless.

Vanauken wonders if we would really want a world like that. No one could choose to bark at his mate, cheat on his taxes, hit someone in anger. People wouldn't choose to be good—they would have to be. God would have taken back his original gift— freedom.[16]

Suffering as Freedom

The murders in your city last week, the shooting down of KAL *107* by the Russians, the drunken driver who killed a child—these all involve the freedom of persons to choose. Since we're not automatons, we treasure choice as one sacred ingredient of being human. Paula D'Arcy, whose books *Song for Sarah* and *Where the Wind Blows* deal with the meaning of her life after the tragic death of her husband and daughter, writes reflectively on Vanauken's essay: "The gift God gave to man was the freedom to choose. If God acts to prevent the consequences of choice, the gift is withdrawn . . . to finite man, what meaning can goodness have if there is no badness?" She then adds, "How can a God of love allow such dire consequences as freedom breeds?"[17]

The answer lies in understanding that God doesn't define love as the absence of pain. A God of love also suffers as humans use their freedom to cause a child to suffer, or to make another human miserable, or even when he sees us heap burdens on ourselves that are too heavy to carry.

D'Arcy thinks we should get on with living, for "life is as it is." But she also notices that "All such suffering, result from personal freedom, the freedom He gave. They are consequences of freedom wrongly used. And if He were to interrupt that, He would interrupt the order of the universe which He established."[18]

The difficulty arises, however, when it seems that God does interrupt the order. Take my case. I was dying of cancer until God interrupted or intervened in the process. Then the question becomes "Why me? Why not others? When will he and when will he not?"

There is no formula. If there were, humans could punch the buttons and control God. Fairness is a human perspective, not a divine one. I've heard, "How could God stand by and not do something" on many occasions when I agreed with the questioner. We need to pause and reflect, however, on the fact that we've been given the intellectual ability and freedom to pursue questions like this. Our freedom is properly called "the perilous gift." As Victor Frankl observed: man could invent the Auschwitz gas chamber, but he could also enter it with a prayer of trust on his lips.[19]

B. W. Woods in *Christians in Pain* writes: "God has allowed this freedom. Man holds in his hands the possibility of good and evil . . . Man develops atomic power, and uses it for bombs. His capacity for love is offset by his power to hate."[20]

Woods suggests that there are two aspects to God's will – the permissive and the purposeful: the things God allows to happen and the things he causes to happen. This view permits God to put up with what man chooses to do that is evil or what Satan chooses to do that is destructive and contrasts that with what God does on purpose. According to this reasoning, God's purpose can be thwarted, although temporarily.

My biggest problem with this view is that we (meaning humans) created these categories arbitrarily. When Job's life tumbled in, which was it—permissive or purposeful? More important, would it have made any real difference to Job? Would it have helped him to know? Would it help any suffering person today? Those I seek to encourage don't get any comfort from thinking about whether God caused their suffering or allowed it. They usually consider it a difference without a distinction.

Suffering as Interdependence

We humans do not live in isolation but in mutual interdependence with each other and the natural physical world around us. Parents, friends, and environment all contribute to the quality of our life. "None of us lives. . .[or] dies to himself" (Rom. 14:7). Even heredity is part of this interdependence. For example, my teenage son is dyslexic. As his adoptive parents, we were not surprised to learn that his birth father was also dyslexic. This is a genetic trait passed on to a son he has never seen. This interconnectedness, genetic and social, makes us all vulnerable to various forms of suffering.

Paula D'Arcy observes, "The interconnectedness of all living things is both beautiful and frightening."[21] I think first of relational stress such as absentee parents, deep-seated animosities in families, parents who suffer with and over their children who are handicapped in one way or another. Relationships involve great risk, and there is always a high probability that we will hurt someone we truly love. Suffering is an inevitable part of our interdependence.

In the physical world the interconnectedness is delicate, even fragile. Consider the fine harmony within the cells of the human body. Cells which get out of sync create the suffering we know as cancer.

If we recognize the delicate interdependence between us and our world, we gain further understanding of the sources of our suffering. However the questions remain: Does anyone care? Is anyone really in charge?

The Inscrutable Purpose of God

Our inability to fathom the depths of suffering is really just another part of being human. In Scripture there are partial answers, but finally we throw up our hands and say, "God knows and I don't." The knowledge of suffering's place in the scheme of things is God's to possess. That's why it is absolutely necessary that we know what kind of God we have.

Martin Luther translated Jeremiah 29:11, "I know what kind of thoughts I have concerning you, says the Lord: thoughts of peace and not mischief."[22] That's why the Old Testament describes believers trusting their suffering, with its hidden meaning, to God. Our explanations are an honest, but inadequate, quest, and if we add up *all* the explanations, they still give only a partial answer. Which brings us full circle to the beginning of our life as believers: *the nature of biblical faith is trust.*

Our Response to Partial Answers

What happens to us when we experience suffering or adversity may not be as important as the way we respond to it. A number of physicians, theologians, and writers have given close examination to this matter, both in their own lives and the lives of others. Through this they have noted some definite patterns in the way we respond.

In her early research on dying patients, Dr. Elisabeth Kubler-Ross identified common stages in the process of dealing with death: denial, anger and rage, bargaining (with God), depression, and a sense of worthlessness. These stages are remarkably similar to the common responses to other kinds of suffering.

Walter Bruggemann also developed this theme, showing that human responses to adversity exhibit some "universals."[23] In their study of human loss and grief, Kenneth Mitchell and Herbert Anderson point out that there are some "necessary" ingredients that we find in all human experiences of pain. In other words, we act this way when we suffer because we are human.[24] I want to give a brief sketch of seven ways we respond.

We try to avoid suffering

Our natural human reflex is to flee from what we know will hurt. Thus, we try to avoid suffering in any way we can. Several Old Testament figures give us good examples of this reaction: Jacob (Gen. 27–41 ff.); Moses (Exod. 2:11 ff.); David (1 Sam. 19–21); and Elijah (1 Kings 19:3–4).

We become paralyzed by suffering

Horrible suffering can bring us emotionally and literally to our knees. Fear and shock paralyze us so that we are unable to think or act rationally. An extreme example of this is Eli, the priest of Israel. When he learned about the death of his sons and the loss of the ark of the covenant, the shock caused his death (1 Sam. 4:12–18).

We fight back against suffering

Another basic human response is the desire to fight adversity with all our strength. This can range from an outcry of agony and a call for help (Gen. 27:34; 2 Sam. 19:1–4) to extreme anger that fuels a desire for physical revenge (Gen. 4:23–24).

We adjust rationally to suffering

Knowing our bad choices have brought us pain, we have the capacity to choose other, better courses in the future. Thus, when faced with a choice, we reflect on the course of action that has caused us hurt in the past and adjust accordingly. We act rather than react.

We transform our suffering

Sometimes we can take the fact of suffering and draw specific meaning from it for our lives: it is an attack of Satan; it is a message from God; it is an occasion for getting to know God better. When we do this, we mentally marshal our faculties to the "battle."[25]

We resign ourselves to our suffering

In her book *Affliction* Edith Schaeffer, widow of Francis Schaeffer, talks about this response as "sitting-in-the-corner-until-it-happens." Rather than biting our lip, gritting our teeth, or slumping our shoulders with eyes closed until it's over, she suggests we adopt a view of patience that is both expectant and hopeful.[26]

We trust God with our suffering

Elisabeth Elliott, whose first husband was killed by the heathen Auca Indians in Peru and whose second husband died of cancer, says: "Because God wills me joy, I will trust Him with my tragedies."[27] This is the response of true biblical faith, but it is not a response that comes naturally to many of us.

Rabbi Alexander Steinbach in *Through Storms We Grow* says that since suffering awakens the human spirit, we can't be fully human if we resign and follow the course of least resistance. But rebellion through fighting back can lead to cynicism and a bitter spirit. Instead, he suggests "cooperation"—a response that seeks to work with partial understanding by placing meaning on our setting so that our hearts live courageously. Then we can understand what is most important in life and, through trust, live gracefully.[28] I've seen many people respond this way, but I've also seen others respond with despair.

Rabbi Harold Kushner observes: "I have seen some people made noble and sensitive through suffering, but I have seen many more people grow cynical and bitter."[29]

4

What Job Teaches Us

The story of Job doesn't tell us why there is disease, war, and tragedy. It doesn't explain why some babies are born healthy and others not, why some people die of cancer in their twenties and others live to be ninety. But Job's story has been studied for centuries for clues about God and his relationship to suffering people. "Job's name is synonymous with suffering. This is why we are attracted."[1] I want us to look closely at Job for two reasons: to try to see God more clearly, and to understand the human being who is suffering—Job, especially as he relates to God.

When adversity strikes, Job is living in the land of Uz. He fears God; he shuns evil; he is blameless and upright. He has seven sons, three daughters, and thousands of animals. He's prosperous. He fits the conventional wisdom of his day which says that he is prosperous because he does right. People who do right are blessed; people who do wrong are punished.

Then one day while Job is enjoying all that God has given him on earth, something happens in heaven that will forever change that. The angels come and present themselves before God, and Satan joins them, apparently uninvited. The Lord asks him where he has come from, and Satan replies that he has been wandering to and fro on the earth.

"Oh," says the Lord. "While you were there, did you take a look at my servant Job? There's no one on earth like him. He's a man who fears me and shuns evil."

"Does Job fear you for nothing?" Satan replies. "Haven't you put a hedge around him and his household and everything he owns? You have blessed the work of his hands so that his flocks and herds are spread throughout the land. But if you stretch out your hand and strike everything he has, he will curse you to your face."

"Very well, then," God says to Satan. "Everything he has is in your hands. But don't lay a finger on the man himself."

Satan leaves and begins afflicting Job. Soon, through a series of disasters, Job's flocks and herds are destroyed and his sons and daughters are killed. Everything is taken away from him—not only his possessions, but also his relationships with those he loves and cherishes. But even in the misery of his lonely, meaningless suffering Job does not curse God.

Once more Satan presents himself before the Lord in the presence of the angels. And again the Lord asks him, "Have you considered my servant Job?"

"I've considered him," Satan says. "But let's bring in a new dimension. A man will give everything he has for his own life. If you'll stretch out your hand and strike Job's flesh and bones, he'll curse you to your face."

"Very well, then," says the Lord. "He's in your hands. But you cannot take his life."

So Satan afflicts Job with painful sores from the soles of his feet to the top of his head. And Job's wife says to him, "Are you still holding on to your integrity? Curse God and die!"

Up to this point, Job has not sinned "with his lips" (Job 2:10). Yet he doesn't know why he's suffering. He doesn't believe it's justified, for he is convinced he has done nothing wrong. He believes that if he could get an audience with God, then God would explain these things to him. Haven't you ever wanted an audience with God when things go wrong in your life?

If God Would Just Explain

A few years ago someone gave me C. S. Lewis's book, *God in the Dock*. In it Lewis says that modern man wants to put God on trial and get him to answer questions about the way he runs the world. If God answers our questions to our satisfaction, then we will trust him, believe in him, worship him, serve him.

> Ancient man was more afraid than that. He may have had his questions, but he didn't think it was right to come to deity to ask them. We not only rush in to ask them, we want to set the time for the appointment and we want God to come and vindicate Himself. If God should have a reason that is defensible for being the God who permits war, and poverty, and disease, then we're ready to listen to His explanations. And if He has good enough explanations we might even acquit Him. But we are the judge and jury – God is the defendant.[2]

C. S. Lewis was right. We do want answers. Sometimes we don't want them because we're angry, but because we're anguished. Job wanted answers because of anguish and pain and because he believed God was just. His unspeakable pain and his rock-hard faith made him seek God's face.

I'm not sure that Job was wrong to want answers. In fact, later in the book when God comes with accusations against Job's friends, he doesn't accuse Job of being wrong for wanting answers. In spite of this, however, Job seems left with as many questions at the end.

I spent many years believing that the Book of Job was all about suffering. I now believe it may be much more than that.

Susan Sontag wrote a book entitled *Illness: A Metaphor for Life* in which she points out that when we suffer pain and loss, we find within that pain and loss the very meaning of our life. We don't find it in our joys. We are not brought together,

typically, by all the things that make us happy. We are brought
together by the common struggle, by the things that disappoint
us, discourage us, tear down our spirits. More importantly, we
are brought to God.

This is what happened to Job, and it is what happens to us.
We are, in many ways, Job's sons and daughters. Job wanted
answers; we want answers. Yet how can he be an encouragement to our faith when we have more questions when we finish
than when we started?

That's why I think Job is not primarily a book about suffering. It's a book about faith.

God Answers Job

Chapters 38 through 41 of Job deal with God's "answers" to
him. These answers don't explain everything to Job, but they do
explain the most important thing: who God really is.

Dr. John Willis has written: "God does not come to Job to
answer his questions by explaining the reasons why he was
suffering, or to debate with him in a court sense, or because
God's conscience finally hurt him so badly that he was ashamed
not to appear. Job thought he deserved an explanation for God's
behavior, a logical reason for his severe suffering. What he
really needed was a comprehension that God is wiser and more
powerful than any man can ever hope to imagine."[3] (That's very
important for us to see also. The comprehension that God is
wiser and more powerful than any of us can ever imagine is the
new vision that will give us fresh comfort, consolation, and
great peace.)   *an*

What Job needed was a deeper faith *in God as God*. What he
needed most was not an answer to his questions but an un-
wavering assurance that he could always depend on his Creator
in all circumstances. Basically God told Job, "I am God and you
have a decision to make." He asked Job, "Where were you when
I laid the earth's foundations? Tell me if you understand. Who
marked off its dimensions? Surely you know. Who stretched the
measuring line across it, or on what were its footings set? Who

laid its cornerstone?" Rather than a put-down, this new per-spective was intended to restore Job's confidence and renew his hope.

The Lord proceeded to help Job understand what he could know by pointing out what he did not know. He did not know the ways of God. Because of this ignorance, God had to help Job by showing him his glory.

When Job asked for someone to talk to, God presented him-self. And at the end of that discussion Job replied to the Lord,

> I know that you can do all things; no plan of yours can be thwarted. You asked, "Who is this that obscures my counsel without knowledge?" Surely I spoke of things I did not under-stand, things too wonderful for me to know. You said, "Listen now, and I will speak; I will question you, and you shall answer me." My ears had heard of you but now my eyes have seen you. Therefore I despise myself and repent in dust and ashes (Job 42:1–6 NIV).

Job finally understood that he must let God be God.

You and I face the same crisis Job faced. Most of us can't identify with the extreme disasters that befell Job all at once, but we may have that tragic accident that we can't explain. That difficult illness that wiped us out emotionally. That lost job. We have people who tell us they don't love us any more and walk away. We're left to rear children knowing that we're not prepared, knowing that we need help, that we're inadequate. So we look to heaven. Maybe not with clenched fists, but with great anguish of heart. "Why, God? Why? Why me? Why this? Why now?" we cry. We not only don't like what happens, we also don't like when it happens and to whom it happens. We don't like anything unpleasant. We don't like anything that's pain-ful. What does God have against me, we ask.

Most of the questions we ask in our tough situations relate to the character of God. First, we'd like the situation changed, of course. But after that we want to know: "Who is this God? Is he a good God who loves me, or is he a capricious God who plays with his creation? Does he have a purpose for what he does, and if so, why doesn't he tell us what it is so we don't feel blind-sided?" We don't want to just know that he cares. We want to know if his care has any teeth in it. Is he going to do anything about our circumstances?

That's where we encounter our greatest problem. We're ask-ing God to change circumstances that we don't understand. We're asking him to view the situation in the limited way we view it. We have no idea, so many times, what his purposes are. We read Scripture and we know that "in all things God works for the good of those who love him" (Rom. 8:28 NIV), and we are puzzled. It doesn't say that everything that happens is going to be good. It says that God is going to work in all those circum-stances, however miserable they are. We know this to be true, but we find limited consolation in it.

We don't like bad things happening to good people. Even when we acknowledge that we're not good people, we don't like bad things happening to us. We don't like anything in our way, and that's the crux of our problem—we want it our way! We want God to come down and give us his reasons. If we agree with his plan, we'll submit to it.

We just don't understand. Through the centuries God has at times given announcements and visual aids (I'm referring here to Jesus). He has not given explanations. Fortunately, what he has said is marvelously loving because of what he has done. If he hadn't given his visual aids, his announcements would ter-rify me.

From time to time our limited point of view causes us to question whether or not God is worth obeying. Abraham was told, "Get up and get Isaac, and this is what I want you to do." From a superficial reading of Abraham's story in Genesis 22 we might think that the patriarch marched out there to sacrifice his son without hesitation. But Abraham was a human being; he must have been in anguish. Did he march out there think-ing, "I don't understand how this is going to work. It seems to thwart all the things I know about the plans of God." Talk about a crisis of faith! How did he get Isaac to lie still as he tied him up? Did he have to trick him? Or did Isaac just say, "Whatever, Dad. If you want to sacrifice me, go ahead." I have an idea that it wasn't pleasant. Abraham must have wondered up until the time God stopped him how in the world this was going to serve God's good purposes.

Like Job, Abraham encountered the living God and passed the test. He chose to obey.

When we say Satan is alive and well on planet earth, we mean that he's still saying, "How can you believe God? You don't even know what he's doing. These things that are happening to you—can you still say God loves you? God doesn't love you or your daughter wouldn't have died. . . If God loved you, you wouldn't have lost your job. . . If God loved you, the one you've pledged your life to wouldn't have left you."

Satan is still very alive, very well. He says to us, "Are you just going to trust out of raw faith? This God you say brings rain to you—he brings rain to the wicked people, too. Is that the God you trust? He does these things to everybody. You're not special."

In the presence of suffering, the issue is faith. In moments of anguish, the issue is more than our pain; it is our God. Is it easy? Was it easy for Job to go against his wife's counsel? She was the only one he had left; and she had some reasons to feel bitter. He stood in the darkness with the whispering of the wind and said, "Everything I see doesn't add up to this conclusion. But I'm going to look beyond what I can see. I have decided to believe God." He had decided, "Though he slay me, yet will I hope in him" (Job 13:15 NIV). Our point of view is limited, but a decision of faith says that the sovereign God knows what he is doing. Job can be a very encouraging book.

In *What Do You Say to Job?*, Kathryn Lindskoog, an insightful writer who battles multiple sclerosis herself, wrote that the world will always have Jobs and will always have Job's comforters. She adds that sufferers are encouraged because Job "fought like a tiger. . .[and] exposed his sensitive feelings"; but mostly he cared to know if God was for him or not. "Did God love him?" was the issue.[4]

Dr. James Thompson says that the effect of the forty questions God asks Job is to give overwhelming evidence that God controls all. Even evil is not ultimately beyond His control. God's purposes will be realized. Job is called to trust God. And the divine speeches show Job that God cares enough for him that He reveals Himself to Job in this way.[5]

Thompson affirms that it was God's love that led to wholeness in Job's life. First, God gave Job a new perspective on the past by letting him know that his life was an undeserved gift from God; next, God called the whole justice-injustice approach into question; and finally, God gave Job a fresh vision for the future. Through this Job realized that God could still give meaning to life and that with God, he still had a future with "an enlarged capacity for life."[6]

Carl Jung's *Answer to Job* suggests a startlingly different conclusion. He discusses a "savage" God who, when one of his innocent creatures—Job—wants to know why he suffers unjustly, feels threatened, defensive, and vulnerable to men finding out that he has a bad side as well as a good side. When Job comes to talk about his suffering, he "cannot deny that he is up against a God who does not care a rap for any moral opinion and who does not recognize any form of ethics as binding." The famous psychologist believed "God as experienced, then, must be evil as well as good, unconscious as well as conscious." In his view, God is torn between his goodness and badness and refuses to reason with Job about his justice.[7]

Sadly, Jung describes a God somewhat like the gods of the Greeks, but one that is foreign to the Scriptures. In the end Jung says that Job understands God better than God understands himself. Jung overlooks all textual evidences for the evidence of his personal psychological career. (Jung is fascinated in this work with enantialromia, the interplay of opposites in psychology. His proof is his psychological experience.) I prefer to agree with Abraham Heschel who observed about the whole of the Old Testament, "The God whom Israel worships is not characterized by apathy, but by *pathos*—and by sensitivity to the human condition."[8]

I also agree with Philip Yancey when he says, "No one has expressed the pain and unfairness of this world better than Job." He then goes on to explain Job's victory: "The view behind the curtain in chapters 1 and 2 reveals Job was being exalted, not spurned. God was letting His own reputation ride on the response of a single human being. . . By hanging on to the thinnest thread of faith, Job won a crucial victory in God's grand plan to redeem the earth. . . Job's doubts were silenced by a vision of God answering him from a whirlwind. . .ours too [are] silenced by revelation."[9]

Charles Swindoll, in *Living on the Ragged Edge*, says God's mysteries, especially suffering, defy human explanation because they go beyond human intellect and wisdom. We "lack the eternal perspective." Like Job, we "can't grasp God's plan," and "we don't know when it will reach its goal." But we can say with Job, "Though I am without answers, yet will I believe in Him."[10]

Swindoll recommends that we handle the mysteries that defy explanation by admitting three things. Admit "I am only human"—and admit it daily. Admit "I don't understand why—and I may *never* on this earth learn why." And, admit "I cannot bring about a change."[11]

Is it a cop-out to suggest that Job understood in a way that perhaps we don't "the place of wonder in the life of trust"? Can the mystery of suffering be explained by the mystery of wonder? In asking these questions in *The Color of the Night*, Gerhard Frost says: "Wonder isn't an esthetic treat or spiritual sweet, peripheral to faith. Wonder is central to faith's venture. It is. . .the trusting spirit. Wonder is an emotional and volitional frontier. It leads to broader and deeper levels of commitment and life-participation. . .increased creativity and exploration into God's glory and grace."[12]

5

A Discussion with Rabbi Kushner

Rabbi Harold Kushner is the rabbi of Temple Israel of Natick, Massachusetts. He is also an award-winning author of the best-selling books, *When Bad Things Happen to Good People* and *When All You've Ever Wanted Isn't Enough*. As a theological student, Kushner was perplexed by the Book of Job. In his work as a rabbi he counseled many in pain and sorrow, but he struggled in a way he had never struggled before when he learned that his three-year-old son, Aaron, had a rare, fatal, aging disease known as progeria and would live only to his teens.

Rabbi Kushner wrote *When Bad Things Happen to Good People* so he could give it to people who had "been hurt by life— by death, illness or injury, rejection or disappointment [to one] who knows in his heart that if there is justice in the world, he deserves better." He wanted, he said, not to "defend or explain" God but to "distill some blessing out of Aaron's pain and tears" by trying to console and encourage people trying to believe.

Kushner is, in his own words, "a fundamentally religious man who has been hurt by life."

Aaron died two days after his fourteenth birthday. "This is his book," says Kushner, "because any attempt to make sense of the world's pain and evil will be judged a success or failure based on whether it offers an acceptable explanation of why he and we had to go through what we did...his life made it possible and his death made it necessary."[1]

Kushner wanted people to go on believing, even though he recognized that they may be incredibly angry with God and restless with religion. He also knew that many sufferers were blaming themselves for their own or their loved one's suffering. He was disgusted with the number of books that attempted to defend God's honor through the use of "logical proof that bad is really good and that evil is necessary to make this a good world." I'm sure that some of the partial answers we've discussed would anger Kushner because theory is cold when warm tears are pouring down grieving parents' cheeks. And I do agree with him that we need a message that helps the heart as well as the head.

My friend Dr. Tony Ash teaches university students and is skilled at dealing with the real questions of life. This is what he says about the real question of suffering:

> It is the Christian claim that God is all-powerful, and that He is infinitely loving and merciful. Yet if He is all-powerful, why does He allow suffering? If He cannot stop it, He is not all-powerful. If He can stop it, but will not, how can we say He is loving? If God can make His creatures happy, and does not, how can He be infinitely loving?... if God has the power to keep a [couple's child from being deformed and dying] why doesn't He do it? To have all power and yet allow such a thing to happen seems more the act of a fiend, than of an infinitely loving God.[2]

Rabbi Kushner's Position

Rabbi Kushner takes a different approach. Maybe, he says, God does not cause or allow our suffering. Maybe it is outside of his control, outside of the will of God. He says most of us read the Book of Job and assume that (1) God is all-powerful and causes everything to happen in the world. Nothing happens without His willing it. (2) God is just and fair and stands for people getting what they deserve, so that the good prosper and the wicked are punished. And (3) Job is a good person.

Kushner believes that the author of the Book of Job takes the position that (1) God is good, (2) Job is good, and (3) God is not all-powerful. He says: "Bad things do happen to good people in this world, but it is not God who wills it. God would like people to get what they deserve in life, but He cannot always arrange it. Forced to choose between a good God who is not totally powerful, or a powerful God who is not totally good, the author of the Book of Job chooses to believe in God's goodness."[3]

He cites Job 40:9–14 in establishing his thesis: "Have you an arm like God, and can you thunder with a voice like his?... [you] tread down the wicked where they stand. Hide them all in the dust together...Then will I also acknowledge to you, that your own right hand can give you victory."

Kushner says: "I take these lines to mean, 'if you think that it is so easy to keep the world straight and true, to keep unfair things from happening to people, *you* try it.' God wants the righteous to live peaceful, happy lives, but sometimes even He can't bring that about. It is too difficult even for God to keep cruelty and chaos from claiming their innocent victims."[4]

He also believes the battle God has with the sea serpent, Leviathan, in chapter 41 indicates the great difficulty God has in subduing chaos and evil—the uncontrollable things in this world. He can do it, but he must work very hard at it.

Kushner understands the sense of loss that can occur when one gives up the all-powerful God "who guaranteed fair treatment and happy endings, who reassured us that everything happened for a reason." He says: "When we have met Job, when we have *been* Job, we cannot believe in that sort of God any longer without giving up our own right to feel angry, to feel that we have been treated badly by life."[5]

It is Kushner's conclusion and recommendation at that point that have caused the most discussion:

> There ought to be a sense of relief in coming to the conclusion that God is not doing this to us. If God is a God of justice and not of power, then He can still be on our side when bad things happen to us. He can know we are good and honest people who deserve better. Our misfortunes are none of His doing, and so we can turn to Him for help. Our question will not be Job's question, "God, why are You doing this to me?" but rather "God, see what is happening to me? Can you help me?" We will turn to God, not to be judged or forgiven, not to be rewarded or punished, but to be strengthened and comforted."[6]

We will feel better if we admit there are some things God does not control because we will be free to look to him for the things he can do. Kushner sees what God can do principally as helping us by caring for us.

To explain, then, why the bad things still happen Kushner develops a theory of *randomness in the universe.* He agrees that God created an orderly world in place of the chaos that existed. He says to suppose creation is not finished, that it is still going on. "The world is mostly an orderly, predictable place, showing ample evidence of God's thoroughness and handiwork, but pockets of chaos remain." Then he further develops this. "Most of the time, the events of the universe follow from natural laws. But every now and then, things happen not contrary to those laws of nature but outside them. . .these events do not reflect God's choices. They happen at random. . .another name for chaos, in those corners of the world where God's creative light has not yet penetrated."[7]

He adds, "And chaos is evil; not wrong, not malevolent, but evil nonetheless, because by causing tragedies at random, it prevents people from believing in God's goodness." The tidal wave that recently hit Bangladesh is one example; the Delta plane crash at Dallas airport because of undetected wind shear is another. Although the second law of thermodynamics suggests that the world is moving toward more randomness, Kushner believes that the Book of Genesis holds out hope that God's spirit may be moving in our world, "operating over the course of millennia to bring order out of chaos." Or perhaps God finished his work with a residual chaos that makes things happen according to chance and we'll just have to live with it even though it is "not the will of God" and "stands independent of His will," making him as frustrated and angry as it makes us.[8]

To the why questions surrounding suffering, Kushner says he really hasn't found a satisfying answer. "The best answer I know is the reminder that man today is only the latest stage in a long, slow evolutionary process."[9] Since he believes God can't do all we'd like him to do, the rabbi suggests that what God does best is comfort us in our affliction. He urges us to forgive and love God even after we've found out that "He is not perfect, even when He has let you down and disappointed you by permitting bad luck and sickness and cruelty in His world, and by permitting some of those things to happen to you." If we can accept God as loving but limited, Kushner believes, he will "enable us to live fully, bravely, and meaningfully in this less than perfect world."[10]

Are His Conclusions Biblical and True?

Rabbi Kushner lives in the real world of suffering people and really cares about them when they hurt. But are his views true, dependable, and trustworthy? He says God is a God of justice and not of power. He presents a God who racks his brain to figure out what went wrong with his creation. He's sad, frustrated, and angry over how it turned out, but he doesn't have the power to change it.

Kushner would have God apologize to the agonizing Job and say, "I care but I can't help." Would this have reassured Job, or would it have perplexed him more, deepening his misery?

God's speech to Job was powerful, not apologetic! "God doesn't explain," says Frederich Buechner. "He explodes. He asks Job who he thinks he is anyway. He says that to try to explain the kind of things Job wants explained would be like trying to explain Einstein to a little-neck clam . . . God doesn't reveal His grand design. He reveals Himself."[11]

Philip Yancey also questions Kushner's final conclusion. "If God is less-than-powerful, why does He choose the worst possible situation, when His power is most called into question, to claim omnicompetence?"[12]

Warren Wiersbe, in *Why Us? When Bad Things Happen to God's People*, challenges Kushner's view of the evolutionary progress of men, saying that even if this were true, we couldn't use the words good or bad about events because "the tragedies of life are only helping to lift man higher on the evolutionary scale." Furthermore, evolution can never explain the presence of moral evil in our world, he says.

Wiersbe also takes issue with the view of a "limited God." Humans live by promises and not by explanations, he says; but those promises depend upon the one giving them having the power to fulfill them. "If God is unable to act, then His promises are vain. If God can't back up His promises with His power, then why trust Him? . . . If God is limited and can't intervene in the affairs of the world or your life, then He is unable to judge evil." A limited God can't be trusted to handle the future, for he's not powerful enough to make the decisions now that will determine the future. And, "A God who cannot control the future or the present is not worth praying to, because He is helpless to intervene." A limited God, rather than relieving us, worries us greatly.[13]

Wiersbe finds it intriguing that Job knew nothing of a limited God. "Perhaps the most important thing we can say about Job's faith is that he never doubted the sovereignty of God." The sad thing about Rabbi Kushner's study is that his faith does not take notice of God's personal response to our suffering that took place when he visited our planet. He talks movingly about a God who cares, without reference to his incarnation which most powerfully demonstrates that very truth. "God's greatest – and final–answer to human suffering and the presence of evil in this world is Calvary."[14]

Rabbi Kushner may be a compassionate spokesman about God for humans who suffer, but the proof of God's compassion for me when I suffer is what he accomplished when he came here. Dr. Ash reminds us that in suffering our emotions tend to rise above the "permanent realities" that we know are true, and we can move beyond what we're feeling to those things that we ultimately believe to be true.[15]

Rabbi Kushner may not stay where his heart has led him. He's a good, loving man who has been in the fire. He says the sense of loss still hurts; but to live is to experience pain.[16]

Of course, from a Christian point of view, I hope Rabbi Kushner will come to know the God who struck a final blow at suffering and death when he powerfully resurrected Jesus.

6

Suffering and the God of Jesus

The final and best proof of an all-loving and all-powerful God comes from God himself, what he has said and what he has done. The New Testament writers affirm God's complete identification with a suffering world. The apostle John says it best when he says God became flesh and dwelt among us. Wayne Oates, in *The Revelation of God in Human Suffering*, says: "The core of truth in the revelation of God is that He, in Jesus Christ as Lord, has Himself entered the arena of human suffering, taking upon Himself the form of a servant, fashioning Himself in the likeness of suffering humanity, and humbling Himself to the death. . .[and by becoming man] He effects our redemption."[1]

The Christian affirmation is that far from being aloof, God participated in his suffering world and suffered as a real human being. God tells us about himself when we look Jesus squarely in the face, for God reveals in Jesus' life, ministry, death, and resurrection that "His supreme intention is for the redemption of mankind."[2]

The Gospels tell us that Jesus brought God's final message— that *he is with us*—and that his loving power rescued us as he gave himself for us, conquering sin, suffering, and death.[3] He overcame the rule of Satan, healing those who were oppressed by the devil, "for God was with him" (Acts 10:38).

> Jesus enters this world enslaved by Satan with the authority of God, not only to exercise mercy, but above all to join battle with evil...[his victories] over the power of evil are not just isolated invasions of Satan's realm. They are more. They are manifestation of the dawn of the time of salvation and of the beginning of [the end] of Satan...Every occasion on which Jesus drives out an evil spirit is an anticipation of the hour in which Satan will be visibly robbed of his power.[4] [See Mark 1:23–28; 5:6–10.]

Jesus announces the kingdom, and in doing so reveals that the reign of God has begun—a time when his salvation comes personally to mankind: "The Spirit of the Lord...has anointed me to preach good news to the poor. He has sent me to proclaim release to the captives and...to set at liberty those who are oppressed, to proclaim the acceptable year of the Lord" (Luke 4:18–19).

Dr. Joachim Jeremias says the images used "are all age-old phrases in the east for the time of salvation, when there will be no more sorrow, no more crying and no more grief." In Jesus' day there was a saying that "Four are compared with a dead man: the lame, the blind, the leper and the childless..."According to the thinking of the time, the situation of such men was no longer worth calling life: in effect, they were dead. But now help is extended to those in the depths of despair, now those who were as good as dead are raised to life."[5]

For all those burdened with sin and its inevitable result, suffering, the good news is "God has intervened"; salvation is here through the forgiveness of sins; "God wants to be near you." God has disclosed his nature dramatically as *loving* and in the resurrection makes a powerful display to emphatically pronounce himself "for us."

Edward Schweizer in *Jesus* says, "If it was revealed in Jesus that God is really a God on the side of man, then Jesus is *ipso facto* Lord of creation, because God proved Himself a God on the side of man by the very fact of his desire not to remain alone, but to create a world."[6]

One of the cutting edges in the study of theology today is renewed interest in a "suffering God." Dr. Terence Fretheim has led the way in his book *The Suffering of God*, a careful study of the Old Testament evidence that God has always suffered *with* his creation, and uniquely with man. He concludes: "God's act in Jesus Christ is the culmination of a long-standing relationship of God with the world that is much more widespread in the Old Testament than is commonly recognized. . . God is not a suffering-at-a-distance God; God enters in. . ."[7]

In their book *In His Image*, Dr. Paul Brand and Philip Yancey underline the truth that if we want to discuss the effect human suffering has on God we must "center on the Incarnation, when God Himself lived among us."[8]

Because we see and understand God best when we look into the face of Jesus, we can accurately answer "How does the suffering of people affect God?" by seeing how it affected Jesus. The Gospel writers show how deeply touched Jesus was by people's pain and grief. A major aspect of his ministry was the healing of the sick (Luke 4:18; 7:22). He dealt with his own pain like we do, praying in the Garden of Gethsemane, "Father . . . remove this cup from me," and crying out his feelings of abandonment on the cross. "My God, my God, why hast thou forsaken me?" (Luke 22:42; Mark 15:34). You cannot read the story of Jesus' crucifixion without thinking about God's pain in that event.

When suffering people talk to me about feeling alone and ask me where God is, I always think about where he was when his son died. He was right there, identifying with mankind, going through death *for* us. Talk about a shared experience. Jon Sobino writes: "On the cross of Jesus, God himself is crucified. The Father suffers the death of the Son and takes upon Himself the pain and suffering of history . . . [In this ultimate solidarity with human beings God] reveals himself as the God of love."[9]

Nineteen hundred years later came the Holocaust, when more than six million Jews were murdered. In Elie Wiesel's *Night,* an account of his boyhood experiences in Nazi death camps, he said he would never get over "the first night in camp, which turned my life into one long night, seven times cursed and seven times sealed. Never shall I forget that smoke [of the crematorium]. . . never shall I forget those flames which consumed my faith forever . . . never shall I forget those moments which murdered God and my soul and turned my dreams into dust."[10]

He tells of a young boy being tortured and hanged by the guards. Just before the hanging he heard someone behind him whisper, "Where is God? Where is He?" After the prisoners had watched the half-hour-long hanging of the boy, the voice asked, "Where is God now?" Wiesel's heart spoke out within him: "Where is He? Here He is—He is hanging here on the gallows." He added, "I was alone—terribly alone in a world without God and without man. Without love or mercy."[11]

What does God announce in the face of horrible suffering? The instructions were given: His name shall be called Immanuel, meaning "God is with us." But if God in Christ suffers with the world, and I believe he does, how can we feel that suffering presence?

The answer is the cross of Jesus Christ. That's where we feel it, see it, and embrace it for our own suffering. One writer claimed God's only justification for himself in a suffering world is the cross of Jesus Christ.

God fully revealed how he feels about our pain, and we see this by watching Jesus' feelings and actions, even his own suffering and death. But there is a mystery here. There will always be mystery in our faith.

The Cross of Jesus and Our Suffering

In the face of the most agonizing misery, such as Elie Wiesel depicts so graphically, we ask, "Does Christian teaching have anything that speaks meaningfully to it?" Another who suffered during the Nazi regime was the German pastor Dietrich Bonhoeffer. Bonhoeffer, who was a part of the Christian resistance to Hitler, rejected an opportunity to flee his country and teach theology in a prestigious American university, choosing instead to stay and suffer with his people. He was arrested, imprisoned, and later put to death by the German authorities.

His *Letters and Papers from Prison* and other writings show his own clear understanding of and abhorrence for the Nazi horror; but his determined Christian faith led him to a radically different conclusion from those voiced by Rabbi Kushner or Elie Wiesel about God's relationship to anguished people. Bonhoeffer believed in a suffering God who suffered on behalf of and with his people. "It was a good thing to learn early that God and suffering are not opposite but rather one and the same thing and necessarily so; for me the idea that God Himself suffers is far and away the most convincing piece of Christian doctrine."[12]

Bonhoeffer believed that in some difficult-to-comprehend way it was God himself who came into the world and died. He believed Paul's statement: "in Christ God was reconciling the world to himself" (2 Cor. 5:19).

Centuries earlier the prophet Isaiah had foretold the coming of a Messiah who would be a suffering servant:

> He was despised and rejected by men, a man of sorrows, and familiar with suffering. Like one from whom men hide their faces he was despised, and we esteemed him not. Surely he took up our infirmities and carried our sorrows, yet we considered him stricken by God, smitten by him, and afflicted. But he was pierced for our transgressions, he was crushed for our infirmities; the punishment that brought us peace was upon him, and by his wounds we are healed. We all, like sheep, have gone astray, each of us has turned to his own way; and the Lord has laid on him the iniquity of us all (Isa. 53:3–6 NIV).

The Japanese Christian thinker Kitamori, in his *Theology of the Pain of God*, written in 1945, soon after Hiroshima and Nagasaki, wrote: "The heart of the gospel was revealed to me as the 'pain of God'. . . God's anger against sin gives Him pain . . . [but God loves the very people with whom He is angry] . . . [His pain] is a synthesis of His wrath and love. . . [in the cross] the 'pain of God' results from the love of the One who intercepts and blocks His wrath toward us, the One who himself is smitten by His wrath."[13]

If we understood how sin separates us from the God who wants fellowship with his special creation – man – then perhaps we'd understand more about the tension between his wrath and love, his justice, and his mercy. Maybe then Elie Wiesel could understand that God *was* on the gallows with that young boy as sinful men displayed their inhumanity.

A striking statue of Jesus stands high, 2,310 feet, above the city of Rio de Janeiro in Brazil. Called the Christ of Corcovado, it is visited not only by tourists, but also by poor Brazilians from the *favelas* or slums of Rio. They seek consolation and help by religious devotion, seeming to plead, "Come down with us, Jesus, into our destitution and poverty and help us. Be concerned. Do not remain aloof in your splendor up here. Come and restore our faith." Yet the cry of the poor has been heard. As Jesus said. "I came down from glory. I have lived among you and I do live among you. I have demonstrated my love through pouring myself out for you. I know of your tribulation, but be encouraged; take heart. I have overcome the world" (cf. John 1:14; 16:33).

John Stott says, "I could never myself believe in God, if it were not for the cross. In the real world of pain, how could one worship a God who was immune to it?"[14] Even Rabbi Kushner accepts that "Christianity introduced the world to the idea of a God who suffers."[15]

Close your eyes and visit Calvary for a moment. You see a rejected, writhing, abandoned figure on that cross. Nails cruelly pierce his hands and feet. His body has been severely beaten; he is bruised and bleeding. Blood drips from the jagged thorns circling his forehead. But he hangs there willingly (John 10:18).

This is an involved God. From now on all human suffering must be understood in the light of his suffering; it is the source of meaning, hope, and new life for sufferers. When someone cries out, "He doesn't care. He's immune to pain," they are brought to the foot of the cross to see for themselves. "Perhaps suffering poses the fundamental test for theology in our time."[16] If that is true, then God's self-giving, in the cross of Jesus and in his resurrection from the dead, is the place where the test is effectively met.

The cross and resurrection hold the key to the mystery of suffering, and while all doesn't become immediately clear, something occurs there that forever affects human suffering. "The God disclosed to the disciples in Jesus Christ was victorious over all evil. The suffering love that they had encountered in him had triumphed over sin, pain, and death. The ultimate power in the universe is the love of God, and fulfillment of his righteous will is on the way."[17]

In Jesus, God "broke the power of death and showed us the way of everlasting life" (2 Tim. 1:10 LB). Because God is good and his power is stronger than death, believers can have confidence that produces the ability to endure and offers a purposefulness to their suffering experiences.

In *Dark Threads the Weaver Needs*, Herbert Lockyer encourages believers, because of God's action in his son, not to "forget that the pattern we fail to see of our perplexities is up there—a pattern fashioned by divine love and wrought out by divine wisdom."[18] Now, when we don't understand, we can trust because we know who God is and that he is *for* us.

Just this morning I drove to a small Texas town to attend the funeral of the father of a valued co-worker. The man died unexpectedly, and the sudden loss is especially hard on his family. I listened as the minister spoke words of comfort to the family.

"We know John is all right because God loves him so much. God knows we're experiencing great pain because we don't have him with us. But John will have a new body the next time we see him. His was worn out and hurt. His new one won't experience sadness, won't know sorrow, will not encounter pain. We know this because that's what God promised, and we know he'll keep his promises because of what Jesus did for us."

I was witnessing real consolation. The minister obviously knew John and understood the family's grief and loss. He also knew God and had great confidence in who God is. He *knew* God cared. He knew God was going to do something about it; in fact that he already had dealt decisively with death. He was a compassionate man with a compassionate message that was not only comforting, but true!

Why is God silent? Why doesn't he intervene? He has. He has spoken and he has acted. We still experience personal tragedies and calamities that force us to cry from the depths of our heart, but in the midst of our cry we can know that he is present. We are living in the *in-between* time. Our redemption has been secured. We and all creation groan in our suffering as we await God's new day (Rom. 8:18–25). Yet we can know that "God is at the helm of the universe . . . there is firm basis for belief in the sustaining power of God's sacrificial love and in the future to which He leads us.[19]

I believe strongly in personal responsibility—the power of choices. That's why I emphasize that each of us chooses how we will respond when suffering touches us. We can rebel, which leads to cynicism and despair. We can passively resign and wait to die. Or we can trust and affirm the God who has loving purposes. Because of Jesus Christ's life, death, and resurrection I am choosing trust, even in the dark days.

After Jesus cried out, "My God, my God, why . . . ?" he said, "Father, into your hands I commit my spirit" (Mark 15:34; Luke 23:46). In his deepest anguish he called God "Father." His disciples had run away; God had abandoned him; he was dying one of the cruelest deaths ever devised. Yet Jesus still trusted his Father and his purposes in all this.

God's victory over suffering is sure because of Jesus' resurrection. Several writers mention C. S. Lewis's statement in *The*

Problem of Pain: "God speaks to us in our pleasures, speaks to us in our conscience, but shouts in our pain; it is His megaphone to rouse a deaf world."[20] If I could be allowed to disagree with a revered source like Lewis, I would say that God's way to rouse a deaf world is by offering his own pain in the death of his son; and his megaphone announces that he is the risen Lord. When we're hurting badly and hear this news about God, we are drawn to him. Receiving our comfort from him, we then comfort others who are racked by life's hurts.

Dr. Paul Brand, physician to lepers, courageously suggests, reflecting on Hebrews 2:10:

> Until God took on the soft tissue of flesh along with its pain cells just as accurate and subject to abuse as ours, He had not truly experienced pain. By sending His Son to earth, God learned to feel pain in the same way we feel pain. Our prayers and cries of suffering take on greater meaning because we now know them to be understood by Him. Instinctively, we want a God who not only knows about pain, but shares in it and is affected by our own. By looking at Jesus, we realize we have such a God. He took onto Himself the limitations of time and space and family and pain and sorrow.[21]

Suffering a New Way

The apostle Paul who wrote more of the New Testament than anyone, bore his suffering as an honor. In the course of his life Paul was robbed, shipwrecked, beaten, and imprisoned. He was exposed to hunger and cold and was threatened with death. Yet he bore his suffering almost as a badge of honor so that the "life of Jesus" could be seen by others. He was thankful that his message about Jesus was backed up by a credible life (2 Cor. 4:10–12).

In a sense Paul went through what all believers go through. He learned the paradoxes that all Christians learn by dying to self, that we rejoice in suffering—not because it's good, but because of what God does in and through it in our lives.

P. 60

P. 32

From Jesus' resurrection forward, suffering doesn't stop, but it is looked at differently by those who believe. There is a power in suffering and a victory over suffering that Christians experience. Believe me, it is not easy to make the world understand what I've just said. But it's true, nevertheless.

The Scottish minister and university professor at Edinburgh, James Stewart, was well known for his compassionate preaching to sufferers. Building on Hebrews 5:9 he reminded suffering people of some values or uses to which they could put their adversity. "And be very sure of this—no sorrow will have been wasted, if you come through it with a little more of the light of the Lord visible in your face and shining in your soul . . . the creative attitude toward suffering . . . [is to] develop your own character [and] become a source of blessing and of strength to others."[22]

Furthermore, he says, "because of the cross, God is in it [suffering] with you . . . When I look upon the cross [I see] the sufferer hanging there is not just another martyr dying for his faith, but God incarnate."[23] Thus, believers can "count it all joy" when they experience trials because they relate them to their faith in God as Father (James 1:2). Or as Paul says, "In all these things we are more than conquerors through him that loved us" (Rom. 8:37).

Paul says that nothing (trouble, hardship, famine, nakedness, danger, or sword) can separate us from the love of God. "God takes the Great Pain of His own Son's death and uses it to blot up into Himself all the minor pains of our own confinement on earth."[24]

Dr. Paul Brand's specialty in medicine is the hand. When contemplating God's pain on the cross, Brand thought of the hands of Jesus, pierced by a thick spike. He noticed the biblical record says that when Jesus appeared in the closed room after his resurrection, he held up his hands, allowing their scars to prove to the frightened disciples that he was the crucified Jesus. Thomas examined the wounds. Brand then asks:

Why did Christ keep His scars? He could have had a perfect body, or no body, when He returned to splendor in heaven. Instead He carried with Him remembrances of His visit to earth. For a reminder of His time here, He chose scars. That is why I say God hears and understands our pain, and even absorbs it into Himself—because He kept those scars as a lasting image of wounded humanity. He has been here; he has borne the sentence. The pain of man has become the pain of God.[25]

Believers can look to this God who keeps his promises, especially that "in everything God works for good with those who love him, who are called according to his purpose" (Rom. 8:28). That's why William Barclay encouraged troubled Christians to pray, "Help me to be very sure that, whatever happens, I do not have to face it alone."[26]

Paul told Christians in Thessalonica that when they were heavy with grief over the death of loved ones, they grieved differently than those who had no hope. They grieved in light of what God had done in Jesus, with a heavy but not hopeless heart.

Paula D'Arcy says Jesus saw each person's misery from his vantage point on the cross:

Every cry of humanity was heard and died for at that cross. The comfort is left to flow through us [believers] as hands and arms of Christ. . .[he] knew at the foot of that cross that in years to come, in spite of all this—the incarnation, the trauma, millions of those for whom he'd done it wouldn't care or understand. In fact they would blame him for this pain and dare to speak of his lack of love and caring. . .they would say that he abandoned them. . .[he accepted that] and that is the God whom I know and with whom I walk.[27]

Living in the In-Between

The Spirit himself testifies with our spirit that we are God's children. Now if we are children, then we are heirs—heirs of God and co-heirs with Christ, if indeed we share in his suffering in order that we may also share in his glory.

I consider that our present sufferings are not worth comparing with the glory that will be revealed in us. The creation waits in eager expectation for the sons of God to be revealed. For the creation was subjected to frustration, not by its own choice, but by the will of the one who subjected it, in hope that the creation itself will be liberated from its bondage to decay and brought into the glorious freedom of the children of God.

We know that the whole creation has been groaning as in the pains of childbirth right up to the present time. Not only so, but we ourselves, who have the firstfruits of the Spirit, groan inwardly as we wait eagerly for our adoption as sons, the redemption of our bodies (Rom. 8:16–23 NIV).

God has our time in his hands and because we have confidence that he is working his plan, we patiently wait. We long to be with him to celebrate the victory as his children. But we are living *between* the *accomplished fact* of redemption and the time when that redemption will be *fully made known*. We anticipate. We live with real hope. We live by the power of his spirit, which is God's gift to his children. But we live with the *not yet*. There is work for us to do as we live in the church—the redeemed family of God—but we remember that his purposes are being served. What is ahead for us far outweighs the afflictions of the present.

Paul says:

(1) Creation groans because evil, though defeated, still produces suffering. It's in its last gasp. God is going to fully redeem it so it will respond fully to his purposes (2 Peter 3:13).

(2) Christians are God's children and have his spirit, but there is so much more in store for them. "The body of humiliation will be transformed into the likeness of Christ's glorified body, when the whole personality will finally experience the benefits of His redemptive work."[28]

(3) Christians must wait in this hope, "accept the trials of the present, so that by patient endurance they may win their lives."[29]

(4) In today's afflictions God's spirit intercedes to help be-

lievers. Paul knew his hardships had helped further God's work and his pains "were the means by which the power of Christ rested upon him"[30] (2 Cor. 12:9 ff.). Everything was affected negatively by the fall of man through sin—everything is being restored because of Christ. Dr. Everett Harrison says, "Scripture does not tell us much of _what_ that glory will be, but it assures us _that_ it will be."[31] We're given just a glimpse, but one that excites and draws us toward it.

I remember Nannie Lewis Frith, a severely affected multiple sclerosis patient. Her days were filled with limitations because her gnarled hands and legs wouldn't allow her freedom of movement. However, I remember her not for her limitations and physical appearance but for her expectant, soaring spirit. If anyone should have despised the present moment, it should have been Nannie; but she would have none of that. For her the present was a time of purpose, even in the midst of anguish. Her God was a God who, because he guaranteed the future, was powerful enough to fill the present with purpose and joy. She looked confidently to the future when the shackles on her body would be broken, but she believed that "the present time is of the utmost importance" (Rom. 13:11, _Phillips_).

For others, like Carol T., physical pain is complicated by mental anguish. She told me, "My husband and teenage children ignore me because I'm sick and can't do anything for them. They use the house as a stopover place for quick meals and changes of clothes. Their lives go on. They are ashamed of what has happened to me, and they no longer treat me like I have a mind or feelings at all. How can I stand this rejection? I'm no good to God or anybody else." The pain of her waiting is incredibly agonizing. The hours of the day are seemingly endless times in which she wonders, "Why do I have to wait? Where is God's will? There's nothing here but utter darkness."

I spent hours in Carol's living room talking about possible reasons for her suffering. I tried to comfort and console telling her how much God loved her, how Jesus would see her through. She dismissed this rather quickly until I finally said, "Carol, I believe God sent me to you today as a visible symbol of his love.

I believe also, as one who has suffered only a little, that it comes down to this: you've made a decision of your will to trust God, and you are being overwhelmed with feelings of isolation, loneliness, and lack of purpose. Now I'm going to ask you to go a step beyond your own situation. I want to ask you to encourage a cancer patient in Texas who feels the way you do. Send her a short note, and ask God to ease her pain. Be God's person for her time of need, Carol. You can do this while you wait on God for your own needs."

At first she looked at me sternly; then a smile came to her face and she said, "I'll try."

Today Carol is still living in the in-between, still living with enormous rejection; yet she is trying to give love *until*. . . . Life's challenging and draining experiences call believers to depend on the resources of God's spirit to help them wait purposefully until God's *karios*—his eternal timetable—is given.

Helen Keller believed that "so long as you can sweeten another's pain, life is not in vain."[32] This is what we do when we find ourselves, as Bernhard Anderson writes, "living in the interim between the inauguration of God's kingdom and its final realization, between the first break of dawn and the full light of day."[33]

Jesus as Teacher and Example

Jesus was made like us in every respect, so he understands the sufferings of flesh and blood people (Heb. 2:17). He experienced the kind of life situations that caused him tears, and he prayed in those depressing and distressing times of his life (Heb. 5:7). Thus, sufferers can fix their eyes on Jesus because he knows how to be faithful during hard times, and he'll help them endure as they run to win life's race (Heb. 12:1–7).

We can look to Jesus both as mentor and model as we face life's losses. He's not an outsider giving advice; he has been a human being. He really cares. He knows that resources are available to us to help us make it. The late E. H. Ijams loved to say that Jesus gives us "power to survive and surpass." Jesus knows about being rejected by people who used to think we were great. He knows how to deal with people who only want to be with us in order to use us. He knows how to nurture the inner life of the human spirit while our physical bodies are facing limitation and pain. He knows how to return good for evil. He knows how to pray when we're so anxious that we're sweating. He knows all about the "cup of suffering." He not only knows how to live, he knows how to die. And he is willing to teach those who ask him.

Lewis Cassals, in *The Real Jesus*, says that Jesus knew how to trust God and to wait in trust for God to accomplish his purposes. Now he offers each follower a special relationship with God similar to his own.[34] There's no better teacher than someone who (a) knows what he's talking about; (b) has been through it; (c) loves you and is eager to work with you until you can do it well too. That's why Jesus is looked to as the perfect teacher about suffering.

Dr. Neil Lightfoot, in *Jesus Christ Today*, describes the Christians to whom Hebrews is addressed as people in need of encouragement. They had suffered many losses and "hope itself was fading from view."[35] Some felt God had forgotten them and could not be counted on to keep his promises. But, the writer argues, Jesus came to earth to identify with us. He suffered because it was appropriate that a Savior suffer with suffering people. When believers suffer hardships, they have a Savior who really understands what they are going through. He's not like someone who is unable to sympathize with their weakness; he has been through the fire of trials and temptations (Heb. 4:14). In fact, "although he was a Son, he learned obedience through what he suffered" (Heb. 5:8). "Although a Son, He still had to suffer. This was a consequence of His incarnation and an essential qualification of leadership."[36] He can lead us because he is especially qualified. He knows how to do God's will through submission in hard times, even when he'd prefer to do something else. He accepted a terribly bitter death—the worst suffering—as his Father's will. And because of his willing suffering, Jesus now has the power to be the source of salvation to us (Heb. 5:9).

Paul said: "Therefore God has highly exalted him and bestowed on him the name which is above every name that at the name of Jesus every knee should bow, on heaven and on earth and under the earth, and every tongue confess that Jesus Christ is Lord, to the glory of God the Father" (Phil. 2:9–11). So Jesus, who offered himself willingly as sacrifice for man's sin, is Lord. He understands the human situation totally. Lightfoot writes that the Hebrew writer: "purposely exposes the grim reality of Jesus' sufferings. He points to Gethsemane; for if ever there was a time when Jesus was surrounded with weakness, it was there. There he urgently prayed that death's cup might be withheld. But if this had been granted, he would not have been like his brothers [us] in all respects."[37]

Jesus didn't have it easy. He knew severe suffering. He cried out for relief. "He suffered as few men have been called upon to suffer."[38] He trusted God when it was dark and he didn't fully understand. That's why I accept him fully as my teacher and my example in many areas, but especially in suffering. He knows the secrets to endurance. That's why I'm carefully studying him.

Peter told suffering Christians, who certainly felt life was unfair, that the way Jesus suffered was an example to them:

> But if you suffer for doing good and you endure it, this is commendable before God. To this you were called, because Christ suffered for you, leaving you an example, that you should follow in his steps. He committed no sin...When they hurled their insults at him, he did not retaliate; when he suffered, he made no threats. Instead, he entrusted himself to him who judges justly. He himself bore our sins in his body on the tree, so that we might die to sins and live for righteousness; by his wounds you have been healed (1 Peter 2:20–24 NIV).

I have received hundreds of letters like the following from cancer patients who feel they are suffering unjustly.

I can't understand why I am in this condition. And other people in the world free, drinking, gambling and other wrong doings, not being Christian and never sick. *Charlene P.*

I know the pain and depths [that] despair and hopelessness can throw us into. Especially when it seems our battles are endless. . . I want to shake my fist at God and say, "Why? Why do you let your servants suffer? We who love you and are so loyal. You have the power to protect us. Why don't you? Why?" *Julie T.*

I shook my fist at God for standing quietly by while the substance of my life was squeezed from me like the squeezing of the inside from a grape. I was angry because the heart of my life was gone. I despaired because the taking was permanent. *Jim V.*

What do we say to them? I say: God understands how you feel. Innocent suffering drains the life from all of us. But God cares about your suffering and the suffering of those you love, and he has done something about it. Trust him. God will vindicate you. He will do justice as his plan comes to full development. Look to Jesus. He will give you the grace to make it through. He will show you a way through your suffering. He suffered and died not only to provide salvation, but to establish *a way to live* in a suffering world.

(1) God knows you are innocent and suffering unjustly.

(2) Jesus' suffering is a model or pattern to be copied.

(3) Yes, it is unjust, but you can trust that God will make it just one day.

(4) Don't retaliate. Control your tongue and trust. The innocent must also be patient.

(5) Remember, Jesus died for you to be able to live this way.

What You Can Do with Your Suffering

If we follow Jesus as teacher and example, we learn the vital place that certain friends of the faith have in the life of those who suffer. We also discover that there are enemies of the faith.

Friends of the faith include praying, careful reading of God's promises in Scripture, being a serving part of the body of Christ in a local church, and seeking out one or two other believers to share with honestly.

Chief enemies of the faith are excessive self-pity, isolation from other believers, inactivity when Christian service is physically possible, constant anxiety, refusal to pray honestly, and inattention to the Father's written Word.

We will not survive if we neglect these friends of faith and encourage the enemies. I've often recommended to hurting people that they can overcome the feelings that "God doesn't care; he isn't near me" if they read anew the story of the cross and resurrection—the greatest statement of his care and action on behalf of the downhearted.

Dr. John T. Willis, in *God and Man, Then and Now*, suggests that we can use suffering to remind ourselves that "real power and wisdom reside in God and not in [ourselves]," that we are "weak and frail and dispensable" leading us to humbly seek God and his consolation.[39] He reminds us that our basic problem is pride and self-sufficiency.

Dr. Willis is my longtime friend, and we now serve as fellow shepherds in a local church. When I became ill with cancer in 1973, he was the only friend who thought to mention this possibility to me.

> "It is quite conceivable that people of God might have spiritual weaknesses or unconscious sins in their lives, which suffering alone could help bring to their consciousness or reveal their true nature and thus help them overcome...thus the child of God should not view suffering as God's means of hurting him or putting him in his place or getting back at him, but rather as the divine method of molding him into a better servant"[40] (see Heb. 12:9–11; Isa. 1:25–26; Mal. 3:1–3).

John says that although a man may not know why he suffers, and it may appear to be unjust, he can believe that God knows what is best and therefore trust his life to him in spite of the way things look. The real test of faith comes when one must believe in spite of the apparent evidence.

I shall never forget the sleepless nights sitting in my living room chair thinking about cancer, chemotherapy, small children, death, suffering—all the time talking to myself about what might be the chastening purposes God had for my illness. I felt convinced that there was purpose in it, a conviction I feel even more strongly today; but I really didn't know what it was. Did the Lord want me to be more serious about him? Did he want me to be more compassionate to hurting people? Was I not clearly seeing the truly important things of life?

After several months I finally decided to accept my illness as a chastising from God in my life and applied the meaning of the chastening as a loving Father's interest in me. I still don't fully know "why," but I've sought meanings that he might have for me, including some I haven't mentioned here. I believe Christians who suffer should not overlook the chastening hand of God. To seek to understand, asking for his wisdom, seems spiritually responsible to me.

I don't know many suffering believers who have it all together, in the sense that they don't struggle from time to time with doubts. However, my reading of the Psalms and the life of Jesus convinces me that struggling with doubt is far from unhealthy; in fact, it may be a good sign that we are seeking an honest, reliable faith.

I also want to add a word of encouragement to those who sometimes feel, "It's not true," or "God isn't here." Don't be shocked by your wavering. Admit it. God isn't shocked; and I'm convinced that he isn't disappointed in you. Wrestle with your faith and your doubts honestly. Keep seeking. Remember what I said earlier: God can deal with the full range of human emotions.

Disappointment in God isn't a terminal condition. You will come out on the other side after your horrible pain recedes some. You will believe again. And the good news is that your faith will be stronger.

7

Living for Others

Αnd he died for all, that those who live might live no longer for themselves but for him who for their sake died and was raised" (2 Cor. 5:15).

Following Jesus as our example means we will suffer on behalf of others. Rabbi Kushner says that after the death of his son, he faced the danger of spending the rest of his life protecting himself against the hurt and pain of loss. But if he did that, he faced a greater danger: the danger of becoming less than a human being. For Christians, the incarnation—God leaving glory to come and die for a suffering world—leaves us no choice but to suffer *with* others. It is his way, his nature. To tell one human that we don't care is to violate our relationship and dishonor our Father. Remember what the apostle Paul said. Praise be to the God and Father of our Lord Jesus Christ, the Father of compassion and the God of all comfort, who comforts us in all our troubles, so that we can comfort those in any trouble with the comfort we ourselves have received from God (2 Cor. 1:3–4 NIV).

There are two common questions on the university campus today: Was I supposed to do something with my life? and, Is there a way to be happy? I want to tell you the truth: If you choose not to feel the pain of your brothers and sisters, preferring to run and hide, you will never know your life's purpose, never be fully human, never know who God is nor be his friend.

I realize those are strong statements, but I believe Jesus has called us to be his active presence in the world. Jesus lives in Christians today and, in us, still suffers for and with the world. In that sense, we represent the gospel. How will suffering people have anyone to sit down and eat with them if Christians don't? The world only kicks them around, compounding their suffering. The "deep meaning of the body of Christ [is that] His hands are not separate from ours."[1] "Lord, when did we see you hungry or thirsty or a stranger or needing clothes or sick or in prison, and did not help you? He will reply, 'I tell you the truth, whatever you did not do for one of the least of these, you did not do for me'" (Matt. 25:44–45).

When a human heart is breaking, I want to be there, for he was there for me. When a crying person asks today, "Is God still love? Does God care about my suffering?" I want to be there. Perhaps my hand on the hand of the sufferer will help the unbearable become more bearable and calm the troubled heart.

Mother Teresa's life work grows out of her compassion for those she calls "a great people among us . . . the unwanted, the uncared for, the rejected, the alcoholics, the crippled, the blind, the sick, the dying–people who have nothing and have nobody." She understands that, "love cannot remain by itself–it has no meaning. Love has to be put into action and that action is service . . . I never look at the masses as my responsibility. I look at the individual. I can love only one person at a time . . . you get closer to Christ by coming closer [to one]."[2] She feels that serving these people helps us understand Calvary.

She adds, reflecting on Matthew 25:

> At the end of life we will not be judged by how many diplomas we have received, how much money we have made, how many great things we have done.

We will be judged by: "I was hungry and you gave me to eat; I was naked and you clothed me; I was homeless and you took me in."

Hungry not only for bread—but hungry for love. Naked not only for clothing—but naked of human dignity and respect. Homeless not only for want of a room of brick—but homeless because of rejection.

This is Christ in distressing disguise.[3]

I must tell you a painful story at this point. While working on this book, I went for long periods of time to a private place, away from telephones and people. For days I would leave my place of work and go "closet" myself to write. On one occasion when I was writing, I heard some bad news about a friend; a great sadness had entered his life. I called someone whom I thought would have the details and asked, "How is he?" The answer, "Pretty shaken." I then inquired, "Do you think I should go?" The answer, "I really think you should. But of course it's up to you."

After the phone clicked, I was overcome by the irony of what had just occurred. A friend suddenly is suffering. I hear about it while jealously guarding my own time—to write a book about suffering and how much God cares. Then my question, with its hint of irritation at having been interrupted, "Do you think I should go?" ("O God, help me be more compassionate!")

The cries of suffering people will always interrupt our peaceful lives. The issue is: Who are we? Are we suffering servants of the suffering servant? I went and spent the morning with my friend and was blessed. We will always have to *choose* to suffer along with others.

The Wounded Healer

We are all "wounded healers." Dr. Henri Nouwen made the phrase popular with his book *The Wounded Healer* in which he described the nature of Christian service in the modern world. Nouwen says a Christian leader must be a person who is able "to make the compassion of God with man—which is visible in Jesus Christ—credible *in his own world.*"[4]

Nouwen observes that what suffering people fear most is aloofness. He says because of Jesus' incarnation, the style of service has been modeled for Christians: we take away someone's suffering by entering fully into it. It may hurt. Listening to someone's story of loneliness or pain can cause us discomfort or ruin our day. But to really care for people, we must suffer beside them. In this way, by being with them in their "alienation or confusion," at the source of their pain, Nouwen says, we can "incarnate the truth" and perhaps represent a hope that offers them a vision beyond human suffering and death.[5] As Christians we are not tied to just optimism when we serve the suffering; we are tied to a God who cares about human suffering and did something about it!

I am a wounded healer—someone who has had to look carefully after my own wounds while at the same time caring enough to try to do something in the name of Christ about the wounds of others. This is the life my Lord teaches me to live and the one he modeled for me. Jesus showed me personal concern and taught me that my neighbor is my brother. Because of my cancer experience, I've been drawn to the world of the sick, lonely, and frightened. I want to use my wounds as a source to lead others' healing, by which I mean that I want them to know Christ and his comfort.

Maybe your wounds are in another area. I have a friend who knows the world of the rejected, those who suffer with low self-esteem. He once lived in that world. But now Christ has given him acceptance—God-esteem—and a mission to those wounded in that area. Another friend specializes with those racked by guilt. I'm not suggesting specialization; rather, I'm seeking to show how we can use the unique experiences of our lives to bless people so that God is honored.

Wounded healers are people who *understand*; they share in the human condition but have great confidence in their God because of the Lord Jesus Christ. "For a deep understanding of his own pain makes it possible for him to convert his weakness into strength and to offer his own experience as a source of healing to those who are often lost in the darkness of their own misunderstood sufferings."[6]

The real healers of the wounds of mankind are those whose own peace has been bought with a price: a valley of shadow, a lonely way, a grim wrestling in the dark.[7]

Letters I've received from cancer patients illustrate something of this truth.

> Thank you so much for your words of comfort!! I very definitely understand all the feelings you have expressed [in *The Gift Of Life*] and I'm still having a lot of them . . . as you say, without God it [cobalt and chemotherapy] would have been almost unbearable. *Evelyn W.*

> Words can't express how much I appreciate your phone call. How comforting it is to know that there are others who share some of my same feelings . . . I have found such comfort in your writings and wanted to share it. I'm relieved to find out that it's okay to be weak sometimes. No more guilt! I owe that to you. *Mary I.*

> Here I am again—early in the morning and sleep has left me. I guess I'm at grips with God again [she had read my book of prayers, *Coming to Grips with God*]. I'm crying out again this morning while the whole world sleeps and I'm here alone . . . I appreciate somebody understanding the loneliness of this struggle I'm going through. I try not to let my true feelings show to my dear husband . . . I feel so much better now . . . I feel almost as if I've been talking with you. When I get to feeling really down I think of you . . . It helps . . . You've helped me through such lonely times. *Shirley W.*

So many in our world are waiting, not for some great deed of kindness or heroic act of service, but for a small signal that we know they are alive. It may be a warm smile with direct eye contact or some word of encouragement we actually mean. At the drive-in window of the bank today the teller told me about her friend's frightening experience of having her house burglarized two days in a row, then sitting alone in her home the next night and seeing two men burglarize the house next door. She is gripped with fear and wants someone to care about her.

I know you are only one person among a number of suffering people. You will grow weary. You will need to retreat for rest and refreshing. However, a life poured out as a wounded healer is one God won't allow to stay depleted. Paul said, "what has happened to me has really served to advance the gospel" (Phil. 1:12). We who have received and are receiving comfort from God find great joy in sharing that comfort.

I've been asked, "Are you prepared to thank God for having had cancer?" The one asking was taking special note of the work of the Caring Cancer Ministry which Camilla and I coordinate. My answer causes me to remember fondly what the late Dr. Batsell Barrett Baxter said about human suffering: "Anything that brings me closer to God, I would have to say, is good for me."

While that answer is not an unqualified yes, I think I understand what Dr. Baxter was thinking. His first cancer experience occurred in 1964 when he was a Bible professor at David Lipscomb College in Nashville. I was one of his students in a sophomore class on "The Minister's Life and Work." He missed three months of the class. Upon his return I listened to him with renewed interest as he spoke of his suffering experience.

Dr. Baxter felt he had been spared by God and was determined to tell young ministerial students to use their opportunities to the fullest to preach Christ. He told us to obtain regular medical check-ups. I remember also his unusually compassionate comments about ministering to the suffering and grieving. A hallmark of his life was his compassion for others. He entered into the hurts of others like no other professor I ever had. A few years later he moved from being my professor to being my co-worker in the Herald of Truth ministry, where I was privileged to work with him for fifteen years until his death.

When I think of wounded healers, I think of Dr. Baxter, for he urgently desired that everyone know God and find in him comfort from their affliction. I recall sitting in a Detroit, Michigan, hotel room with him one night as he read a booklet I was planning to publish entitled "We're Fellow Strugglers." When he had finished, he handed the booklet back to me and said, "I wouldn't change a word. You are so right. Cancer sufferers need to find something secure that cancer can't threaten—Jesus Christ." Dr. Baxter had learned what pain and suffering really are, and as a result he belonged to all who suffered. Throughout his lifetime of radio and television ministry, he probably preached to more people than any other minister in the Churches of Christ. But he always cared about people not as the masses, but one by one.

Helping Those Who Hurt

We can weep with those who weep by *listening* to hurting people. The abundance of advice columnists and radio talk shows is proof that people will do almost anything to get someone to listen to them. It shouldn't surprise us to know that we can get into another's shoes if we desire to.

Donald Peel, in *The Ministry of Listening*, says creative listening is empathy in action by which some suffering can actually be relieved.[8] Dr. Charles Bachmann says that while sensitivity to people's sorrows deserves training, its basic requirement is desire. We can underestimate the value of our presence in communicating hope to people who grieve. If people are to know that "God does not forsake His children in the most critical periods of their existence," then we need to be with them.[9]

J. B. Phillips, the British scholar who translated the New Testament into modern English and helped many younger people to understand the dynamic vibrancy of God's Word, suffered horribly from mental distress, depression, and anxiety. At various times he was overwhelmed by mental pain.

Vera Phillips and Edwin Robertson tell in *J. B. Phillips: The Wounded Healer* the heartbreaking but deeply inspirational story of how sensitively this man ministered to people whose doubts threatened to destroy them. He developed a worldwide correspondence ministry which guided readers through their struggles. His example and compassion helped many retain and grow in their faith.

Since life's losses are essentially self-defined—what causes you pain might not cause me pain—we must take another's suffering seriously. I once spoke to a large assembly in Tulsa, Oklahoma, about the difficulties of the cancer experience. During the lecture I remarked that one of my lighter moments was watching my small children run around the house wearing the wig I had purchased when chemotherapy had done its work on my hair. I said, "But you know, being bald doesn't bother me at all. In fact it's kind of nice. No problem."

As soon as the lecture concluded, an attractive woman came down the center aisle and introduced herself to me. Then, without pause, she said soberly, "Mr. Becton, I would rather have died than to have lost my hair." Before I could reply, she had turned and walked away. I've never forgotten the pain in her voice. For her, the hair loss was catastrophic.

I believe we can also share our hope. We've settled on the belief, if we're in Christ, that suffering doesn't have to be meaningless because God shared it in Jesus. Further, we believe that he is with the sufferer. We can serve whatever need we find and share our faith in the Christ who has "borne our griefs and carried our sorrows."

I like Elisabeth Elliott's reminder to the suffering:

> The one thing that the cross does for all time is to transfigure human experience . . . I bring my sins to the foot of the cross and I'm given the righteousness of Christ. I bring my losses and I'm given gain. I bring my sorrows, I'm given joy. I bring the spirit of heaviness and I'm given the garment of praise. I bring my death and I'm given life . . . As those who stand beside those who suffer physically, mentally, emotionally and spiritually . . . we face it and say "This sorrow, this sin, this suffering, this pain, was borne on the cross of Jesus Christ."[10]

There's a Hasidic story about a student who complains to the rabbi that he's depressed. He feels alone because there's illness and hard financial times at his house. He's afraid God doesn't care about him. As they sit talking, the fire in front of them is reduced to a few scattered embers. The teacher takes the poker and stokes the embers into a heap so that soon they burst into a new warm fire.

The rabbi says to the student, "Did you see what happened when I gathered the embers close together? The fire came back to life. When the coals are separated from each other, there is little heat; but when they are together they get warmth, and the fire is renewed. It's the same with people. Alone, we are separated and disconnected and our spirits are in danger of dying. But when we come to each other, we get warmth and comfort from one another and hope is renewed."[11]

The warmth I get from God, who says in Jesus that I never have to suffer alone, is the warmth I want to stoke in other hearts so that the flame of God's love can warm them well.

The prayer attributed to St. Francis is my prayer as well: "O God, Creator of mankind, I do not aspire to comprehend You or Your creation, nor to understand pain or suffering. I aspire only to relieve the pain and suffering of others, and I trust that in doing so, I may understand more clearly Your nature, that You are the Father of all mankind, and that the hairs of my head are numbered."[12]

A Final Word

The late Creath Davis, a psychologist, told hurting people: "If you find God in your struggle, the struggle (as painful as it is) will be secondary. Your life will take on a quality that is indestructible. Your life will richly bless those you touch."[1]

My friend Creath encouraged us to reject running away from life and becoming one of life's victims. He believed we can trust God even as we ask why. Questioning life's fairness and doubting God's love happens from time to time. But we can set our jaw and decide once and for all that we know God is there, that he cares, and that he brought his power to conquer suffering and death in Jesus.

Remind yourself every day:

(1) A loving God is in control.

(2) He is working out his perfect purpose.

(3) Jesus proves that he cares, is present, and has defeated suffering and death with his power.

(4) Our times are in his hands, and he will help us endure as we trust him.

(5) Our future is as bright as the promises of God.

(6) As we – and all creation – groan, his spirit helps us.

Fred Craddock, in *The Embrace of Necessity*, reminds downcast people that when we have no alternatives but to suffer, we still have a choice. Rather than shaking our fist at heaven or developing a heart that's bitter and cynical or whining about unfairness by blaming others, the world, or God, *we can choose our response.*[2]

When the apostle Paul was in prison, facing death – that great enemy of relationships, plans, and hope – he wanted to be out preaching about Jesus. But he wrote a letter to his friends and told them that with no alternatives he still had a choice. "You know, friends, whether I live or die, Christ will be glorified" (see Phil. 1:20–21). *Whether* I live or die. Death had no hold over Paul. He stood and stared death down, and it was death that backed away, realizing that its power had been stripped away by faith. "O death, where is your victory. . . your sting?" (see 1 Cor. 15:55). Thanks be to God; because of him, sin, death, and suffering do not have the last word. Love, God's love, has the final word. The only real answer to death is resurrection – and that answer has been given!

Notes

Chapter 1. *Suffering as Personal Experience*

1. Elie Wiesel, "The Silence of Man and God," in *Against Silence: the Voice and Vision of Elie Wiesel*, ed. Irving Abrahamson (New York: Holocaust Library, 1985), 1:110.

2. Randy Becton, *The Gift of Life* (Abilene: Quality Printing, 1979), 1.

3. Ibid., 23–24.

4. Martin E. Marty, *A Cry of Absence: Reflections for the Winter of the Heart* (San Francisco: Harper & Row, 1983), 49–51.

5. Ibid., 147.

6. Larry Richards, *When It Hurts Too Much to Wait* (Waco: Word Books, 1985), 74.

7. Ibid.

8. Philip Yancey, *Open Windows* (Westchester, Ill.: Crossway Books, 1982), 27–28.

9. Source unknown.

10. Lewis Smedes, *How Can Everything Be All Right When Everything Is All Wrong?* (San Francisco: Harper & Row, 1982), 55.

Chapter 2. *Why Is There Suffering in the World?*

1. S. Paul Schilling, *God and Human Anguish* (Nashville: Abingdon Press, 1977), 9.

2. Ibid., 11.

3. Joseph H. Fichter, *Religion and Pain* (New York: Crossroad Publishing, 1981), 9.

4. Ibid., 19.

5. Ibid.

6. Ibid., 27.

7. C. S. Lewis, *A Grief Observed* (New York: Bantam Books, 1961), 27.

8. Philip Yancey, *Where Is God When It Hurts?* (Grand Rapids: Zondervan Publishing House, 1977), 11.

9. Ibid., 16.

10. Ibid., 181.

11. Ibid., 86.

12. Paul Billheimer, *Don't Waste Your Sorrows* (Fort Washington, Pa.: Christian Literature Crusade, 1977), 31.

13. Ibid., 80–83.

14. Brian Hebblethwaite, *Evil, Suffering and Religion* (New York: Hawthorne Books, 1976.

15. Ibid., 50.

16. Ibid., 53.

17. Schilling, *Human Anguish*, 25.

18. Ibid., 26.

19. C. S. Lewis, *The Problem of Pain* (New York: Macmillan, 1944), 77.

20. Schilling, *Human Anguish*, 30.

21. Walter Kaufmann, *The Faith of a Heretic* (New York: New American Library, 1978), 137, 145.

22. Marcel Neusch, *The Sources of Modern Atheism* (New York: Paulist Press, 1977), 19.

23. Ibid., 19–20.

24. Ibid., 21.

25. Ibid., 219.

26. Ibid., 239.

27. Ibid., 239.

28. Schilling, *Human Anguish*, 34.

29. Ibid.

30. Ibid.

31. Ibid.

32. Bernhard W. Anderson, *Out of the Depths* (Philadelphia: Westminster Press, 1983), 76.

33. Ibid.

34. Ibid., 69.
35. George A. Buttrick, *God, Pain and Evil* (Nashville: Abingdon Press, 1966).
36. Schilling, *Human Anguish*, 58.
37. Ibid., 64.
38. Ibid., 66.

Chapter 3. *The Meaning of Suffering*

1. Paul Lindell, *The Mystery of Pain* (Minneapolis: Augsburg Publishing House, 1974), 54–55.
2. Billy Graham, *Till Armageddon: A Perspective on Suffering* (Waco: Word Books, 1981), 50.
3. Warren McWilliams, *When You Walk Through the Fire* (Nashville: Broadman Press, 1986), 61.
4. Erhard S. Gerstenberger and Wolfgang Schrage, *Suffering*, trans. John Steely (Nashville: Abingdon Press, 1980), 109–110.
5. John Oswalt, *Where Are You God? Perspectives on Our Response to Injustice and Suffering* (Wheaton, Ill.: Victor Books, 1982), 10.
6. Schilling, *God and Human Anguish*, 148–150.
7. Ibid., 146.
8. Hirshel Jaffe, James Rudin, and Marcia Rudin, *Why Me? Why Anyone?* (New York: St. Martin's Press, 1986), 110.
9. Vance Havner, *Though I Walk Through the Valley* (Old Tappan, N.J.: Fleming H. Revell Co., 1974), 30.
10. Walter Kaiser, Jr., *A Biblical Approach to Personal Suffering* (Chicago: Moody Press, 1982), 123.
11. Schilling, *God and Human Anguish*, 147.
12. Ibid., 161.
13. Ibid., 163.
14. Ibid., 184–185.
15. Ibid., 192.
16. Paula D'Arcy, *Where the Wind Blows* (Wheaton, Ill.: Harold Shaw Publishers, 1984), 130.
17. Ibid., 132.
18. Ibid., 132.
19. B. W. Woods, *Christians in Pain: Perspectives on Suffering* (Grand Rapids: Baker Book House, 1974), 25.
20. Ibid.
21. D'Arcy, *Wind Blows*, 35.

22. Gerstenberger and Schrage, *Suffering*, 115.

23. Roland Murphy, *Psalms, Job: Proclamation Commentaries* (Philadelphia: Fortress Press, 1977), 263–275.

24. Kenneth R. Mitchell and Herbert Anderson, *All Our Losses, All Our Grief* (Philadelphia: Westminster Press, 1983), 35–52.

25. Gerstenberger and Schrage, *Suffering*, 125–128.

26. Edith Schaeffer, *Affliction* (Old Tappan, N.J.: Fleming H. Revell Co., 1978), 128–140.

27. Elisabeth Elliott, "A View of Suffering" (Unpublished speech, 1980), 3.

28. Alexander Steinbach, *Through Storms We Grow* (New York: Bloch Publishing Co., 1964), 180–184.

29. Harold Kushner, *When Bad Things Happen to Good People* (New York: Schocken Books, 1981).

Chapter 4. *What Job Teaches Us*

1 Dr. James Thompson, "Does God Help in Time of Trouble?" (Unpublished sermon, Austin, Texas, 1985).

2. C. S. Lewis, *God in the Dock* (Grand Rapids: Williams B. Eerdmans, 1968), 42.

3. John T. Willis, *Old Testament Wisdom Literature* (Abilene: ACU Press, 1982), 74–75.

4. Kathryn Lindskoog, "What Do You Say to Job?" *Leadership* 6:2 (Spring, 1985): 90–95.

5. Thompson, "Time of Trouble," 7–9.

6. Ibid., 11.

7. Mary Wolf-Solin, *No Other Light: Points of Convergence in Psychology and Spirituality* (New York: Crossroads Publishing Co., 1986). As reviewed in *Books and Religion* 14:8 (October, 1986): 4, 14–15.

8. Anderson, *Out of the Depths*, 82.

9. Philip Yancey, "When the Facts Don't Add Up," *Christianity Today* 30:9 (June 13, 1986), 21–22.

10. Charles Swindoll, *Living on the Ragged Edge* (Portland: Multnomah, 1986), 245.

11. Ibid., 248.

12. Gerhard E. Frost, *The Color of the Night: Reflections on the Book of Job* (Minneapolis: Augsburg Publishing House, 1977), 133–134.

Chapter 5. *A Discussion with Rabbi Kushner*

1. Kushner, *When Bad Things Happen*, 5.

2. Dr. Tony Ash, "The Problem of Suffering" (Unpublished sermon, Austin, Texas, 1985), 1–2.

3. Kushner, *When Bad Things Happen*, 42–43.

4. Ibid., 43.

5. Ibid., 44.

6. Ibid.

7. Ibid., 51–52.

8. Ibid., 53, 55.

9. Ibid., 66.

10. Ibid., 148.

11. Philip Yancey, "When Bad Things Happen to Good People," *Christianity Today* 30:9 (August 5, 1983), 23.

12. Ibid.

13. Warren Wiersbe, *Why Us? When Bad Things Happen to God's People* (Old Tappan, N.J.: Fleming H. Revell Co., 1984), 22, 26–29.

14. Ibid., 35, 47.

15. Ash, "Suffering," 6–10.

16. Harold Kushner, *When All You've Ever Wanted Isn't Enough* (New York: Summit Books, 1986), 88–89.

Chapter 6. *Suffering and the God of Jesus*

1. Wayne Oates, *The Revelation of God in Human Suffering* (Philadelphia: Westminster Press, 1959), 26.

2. Ibid., 27.

3. Joachim Jeremias, *New Testament Theology: The Proclamation of Jesus* (New York: Scribner's, 1971), 288–289.

4. Ibid., 94.

5. Ibid., 104–105.

6. Edward Schweitzer, *Jesus* (Richmond, Va.: John Knox Press, 1971), 87.

7. Terence Fretheim, *The Suffering of God: An Old Testament Perspective* (Philadelphia: Fortress Press, 1984), 166.

8. Dr. Paul Brand and Philip Yancey, *In His Image* (Grand Rapids: Zondervan Publishing House, 1984), 283.

9. John R. W. Scott, "God on the Gallows," *Christianity Today* 31:1 (January 16, 1987), 28–30.

10. Ibid., 30.

11. Ibid.

12. Richard Quebedeaux, *By What Authority* (San Francisco: Harper & Row, 1982), 184.

13. Scott, "Gallows," 29.

14. Ibid., 30.

15. Kushner, *When Bad Things Happen to Good People*, 85.

16. Arthur C. McGill, *Suffering: A Test of Theological Method* (Philadelphia: Westminster Press, 1982), 7.

17. Schilling, *Human Anguish*, 274.

18. Herbert Lockyer, *Dark Threads the Weaver Needs* (Old Tappan, N.J.: Fleming H. Revell Co., 1979), 122.

19. Schilling, *Human Anguish*, 279.

20. T. B. Maston, *God Speaks Through Suffering* (Waco: Word Books, 1977), 71.

21. Brand and Yancey, *Image*, 286–287.

22. Warren Wiersbe, comp., *Classic Sermons on Suffering* (Grand Rapids: Kregel, 1984), 95.

23. Ibid., 103.

24. Brand and Yancey, *Image*, 288.

25. Ibid., 291.

26. Maston, *God Speaks*, 92.

27. D'Arcy, *Wind Blows*, 140.

28. F. F. Bruce, *The Epistle of Paul to the Romans* (Grand Rapids: William B. Eerdmans, 1963), 170–173.

29. Ibid., 171.

30. Ibid.

31. Everett Harrison, *Romans: Expositor's Bible Commentary* (Grand Rapids: Zondervan Publishing House, 1976), 93–99.

32. Wiersbe, *Classic Sermons on Suffering*, 125.

33. Anderson, *The Depths*, 69.

34. Louis Cassals, *The Real Jesus* (New York: Doubleday, 1968), 87–113.

35. Neil Lightfoot, *Jesus Christ Today: A Commentary on the Book of Hebrews* (Grand Rapids: Baker Book House, 1979), 36.

36. Ibid., 110.

37. Ibid., 117.

38. Ibid., 230.

39. John T. Willis, *God and Man—Then and Now* (Austin: Sweet Publishing, 1974), 21.

40. Ibid., 22.

Chapter 7. *Living for Others*

1. D'Arcy, *Wind Blows*, 47.

2. Mother Teresa, *Words to Live By* (Notre Dame: Ave Marie Press, 1980), 14–19, 79.

3. Ibid., 80.

4. Henri Nouwen, *The Wounded Healer* (New York: Doubleday, 1972), 40.

5. Ibid., 74–75.

6. Ibid., 89.

7. Wiersbe, *Classic Sermons on Suffering*, 105.

8. Donald Peel, *The Ministry of Listening* (Toronto: Anglican Book Centre, 1980), 33–34.

9. Charles Bachmann, *Ministering to the Grief Sufferer* (Englewood Cliffs, N.J.: Prentice-Hall, 1964), 13–24.

10. Elisabeth Elliott, "God's Purpose in Suffering" (Personal testimony, 1980), 1–11.

11. Jaffe, Rudin, and Rudin, *Why Me?*, 109.

12. Schilling, *Human Anguish*, 31.

A Final Word

1. Creath Davis, *Coping with Tough Circumstances* (Waco: Word Books, 1979), 162.

2. Fred Craddock, "The Embrace of Necessity," Sermon, Thesis Theological Cassettes 9:8 (September, 1978).

Bibliography

Abrahamson, Irving. ed. *Against Silence: The Voice and Vision of Elie Wiesel.* Vol. 1–3. New York: Holocaust Library, 1985.

Elie Wiesel is the foremost writer on the Holocaust. His writings have been edited and gathered into three volumes, offering excellent insight into a suffering people. The Nobel Prizewinning author depicts the agony of suffering people with powerful words and helps those who seek to understand suffering, so that none of us can forget.

D'Arcy, Paula. *Where the Wind Blows.* Wheaton, Ill.: Harold Shaw Publishers, 1984.

Paula D'Arcy's poignant writing shows her painful search for answers in her own situation of pain and loss. This book communicates well the place of trust in the face of the question why. As she has said, "These are my hard-won conclusions...they're from my struggles to walk away from a blood-stained highway by myself and not forever hate life and its author" (140).

Fretheim, Terrence. *The Suffering of God: An Old Testament Perspective*. Philadelphia: Fortress Press, 1984.

Fretheim is a professor of Old Testament at Luther/Northwestern Theological Seminary in St. Paul, Minnesota. This work focuses on the theme of divine suffering and examines carefully the Old Testament evidence that suffering belongs to the person and purpose of God.

Gerstenberger, Erhard S. and Wolfgang Schrage. *Suffering.* Translated by John Steely. Nashville: Abingdon Press, 1980.

Gerstenberger and Schrage collaborated to describe what the Bible has to say about suffering in both Old and New Testament times. It serves as an excellent survey and has been used as a textbook in seminary classes on suffering. Well-written and thorough.

Hebblethwaite, Brian. *Evil, Suffering and Religion*. New York: Hawthorn Books, 1976.

Hebblethwaite surveys the different ways in which religions of the world have attempted to cope with the problem of evil and suffering. His study of comparative religions and insights into the fundamental questions suffering raises are helpful. He writes as a believer.

Hick, John. *Evil and the God of Love*. New York: Harper & Row, 1977.

John Hick's work on suffering raises the fundamental questions about suffering. He deals with them intelligently and with a good understanding of the theology of Scripture about God's place in human suffering.

Kaufmann, Walter. *The Faith of a Heretic*. New York: New American Library, 1978.

Kaufmann, a long-time professor at Princeton, wrote a devastating attack on the Christian faith. His chapter on evil and suffering is must reading for those who desire to fairly hear what the unbeliever does with the Bible material on the subject. Kaufmann must be dealt with by any Christian arguments.

Kreeft, Peter. *Making Sense out of Suffering*. Ann Arbor, Mich.: Servant Publications, 1986.

Peter Kreeft is a philosopher at Boston College. He summarizes ten historic answers to the problem of pain. His use of creative dialogue challenges the question of evil and a sovereign God.

Kushner, Harold. *When Bad Things Happen to Good People*. New York: Schocken Books, 1981.

Rabbi Kushner's compassionate writing has been received well by American readers. His book should be studied to understand the pain of personal suffering and to understand the rationale which seeks to reconcile the love and power of God with the fact of suffering.

Lewis, C. S. *The Problem of Pain*. New York: Macmillan, 1978.

Lewis's work is fundamental for understanding the issues. It has stood the test of time.

McWilliams, Warren. *When You Walk Through the Fire*. Nashville: Broadman Press, 1986.

McWilliams has provided an excellent survey of the Bible as it relates to suffering and a God who really cares. This book is simply, clearly, and carefully written, and it gathers the Bible material together in a useful way.

Schilling, Paul. *God and Human Anguish*. Nashville: Abingdon Press, 1977.

Paul Schilling's book is the most helpful work I have read on the problem of human suffering and a loving God. His knowledge of world religions, literature, and theology combined with his compassionate, faith-filled approach made this book most helpful. Schilling was a long-time professor at Boston University School of Theology and Boston Theological Union. His fairness with the tough questions, combined with his solid faith, are evident in this scholarly work. Highly recommended.

Yancey, Philip. *Where Is God When It Hurts?* Grand Rapids: Zondervan Publishing House, 1977.

Philip Yancey's study of suffering people has been brought together in one volume. An excellent writer. He has prepared an excellent resource to share with suffering people who want to think about the meaning of suffering.